He Knows My Name

My Shattered Pieces

By

Dyland Weather

Title: He Knows My Name

Sub-Title: My Shattered Pieces

Author: Dyland Weather
Published by S.I.T (Stand In Truth Publications)

305 N 21ˢᵗ Ave Hattiesburg, Ms. 39401
http://www.comfortableinonesownskin.com/stand-in-truth-publications-s-i-t/

Credit to Publisher's Team:

Cover: Richelle B

Editor/Proofreader: Kendra Ashcraft Coffman

Formatter: Shoaib Shahzad

Coordinator: Author Barbara White, Prophetess Angela Boutwell, Evangelist Melinda Walker

 All Scripture quotations, unless otherwise indicated, are taken from the Holy Bible, New
International Version®, NIV®. Copyright ©1973, 1978, 1984, 2011 by Biblica, Inc.® Used by
permission of Zondervan. All rights reserved worldwide. www.zondervan.com

Scripture quotations marked (NLT) are taken from the *Holy Bible*, New Living Translation,
copyright ©1996, 2004, 2015 by Tyndale House Foundation. Used by permission of Tyndale
House Publishers, Carol Stream, Illinois 60188. All rights reserved

Scripture taken from the New King James Version®. Copyright © 1982 by Thomas Nelson.
Used by permission. All rights reserved

Quotes by

Robert H. Schuller

Max Lucado

Daily Inspirational Quotes

Christ Religious Inspirational Quotes

Google

ISBN: 9798852187819

Printed in United States of America

Table of Contents

Dedication

As I have been prayerful during the journey of drafting this book, there have been several special people that God has placed in my life for a reason. I am now understanding why. God never makes any mistakes at all, and I have learned how to listen to the spirit of God. I would like to give thanks to the Almighty God, first and foremost, who is the head of my life!

Secondly I would like to start my dedications to my late daughter Donysha and granddaughter Clarisma. They say time heals, but I must admit, time seals. The word seal means a substance that join two things together to prevent them from coming apart or prevent anything from passing between them. I say time seals and not heal because I will never heal from the hole that is in my heart. Nothing could ever fill that void I feel without you both in my life. I have learned to cope, progress, function and move forward but it is a hurt that remain tucked away that will remain there for life. It is so many things went unsaid. I never got to experience what it is like to have a granddaughter from birth to adulthood. I no longer beat myself up and accept the hand I was dealt but life without the two of you is not what I had imagined. I say time seals because nothing could ever separate my love for you. My love is bonded for life here on earth and in the spirit where you are now. The seal that joins us together is a substance called Love. Love is not anything you can touch. It is not tangible that can expire. Love is a strong emotion that ties one heart to the other. My heart is filled with love that is tied to you both. My prayer is to see you again on the other side. Until then, I will keep moving forward with your love sealed in my heart as I journey through this thing called life.

~ He Knows My Name ~

This book is dedicated to you. You are the very reason I had the srenghth to follow through with telling my story. I love you and thank you for the years God gave you to me on this earth.

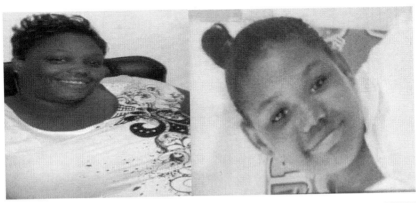

~ He Knows My Name ~

I want to give thanks to my late parents, the Mr. Robert, and Mrs. Nina Weather:.

If it had not been for your love for each other, there would be no me. Thank you for life. Thank you for being with me through thick and thin. Thank you for believing in me when I did not believe in myself. Moma when you were very disappointed in me, you never put me down. I felt the silent prayers and your never ending love. Dad, yes I was the prodigal son that found myself in a pig stine but you always welcome me back with loving arms. Your love for me went without saying. I knew you loved me. I pray you are looking down on my life and are proud of the change that has come over me. God did it for me and your love and direction in life was not in vain. My love is never ending for you as my parents. You are absent in body, but always present in my heart. I love you always.

~ He Knows My Name ~

Thank you to my only living daughter Delilah Weather:

You have been my rock through all of this. Thank you for never folding and always having my back. We have been through some tough times but I learned from you

" Tough times never last, but tough people do."

~ Robert H. Schuller~

~ He Knows My Name ~

A special thanks to my grandsons Nathanial and Michael:

It is a special feeling knowing my legacy will go on forever. All the hard work I put in to make a name for myself will one day be passed down to you. My name will forever live on. Nate, I fought so hard to maintain my integrity after God answered my prayer to spare your life. Life as I know it would really be hard without you in it. Michael I am so glad I did not have to battle for your life, God gave it willingly and my prayer is you never experience what Nate experienced. Through it all, you both shall stand tall in who God called you to be. Granpa Love you and is very proud of you both.

Nate   Michael

~ He Knows My Name ~

To my Emotional Support Animal (Dog) and best friend Tux:

I never thought I could truly quote "Dogs are a man best friend" and truly mean it. Today I can say, you have been a source of strength and peace in my life. I never even knew the impact a ESA could have on one's life until I found myself in a place of anxiety and in need of daily therapy. You provided me with a sense of calmness when all around me and inside of me was raging. You brought a smile to my face many days when I was overwhelmed with sadness and grief. For many years, you helped me get through my grieving process and helped me manage my stress. Thank You Tux for being a part of my sealing and healing process.

~ He Knows My Name ~

Thanks to my entire family and friends:

Lakisha Lockridge, my step daughter, cousin/God brother Darren Remmer, my late friend Leroy Willis, God son Clifton Adams. To my life long friends Calvin Ruggs, Melvin Ruggs, Donnell Shepherd, Trent Towers, Larry Wells, Hugh Boswell, Antonio Brown, Carla Dease, Calvin Pink, Karl Mcneil, and Jeffrey Boxdale. A special thanks to my Business partners who has been through a lot with me, Bob Watson and Donald Watson. To my Prayer Warriors, who happen to be my Aunt's, Youlander Ford, Phyllis Givens, Carolyn Edwards and Diane Taylor.

Thanks to my recovery family, who have understood me and my uphill battles, for most of us have similar commonalities.

Thanks to my mentors: Ferris Thomas, Obie Weathers, Dr. Daryn D. Crenshaw, Pastor Keith Evans, and my sponsor, James Wagner, Pastor Terry Howell and Bishop Lawrence L. Kirby

~ He Knows My Name ~

A special thanks to My Publisher Evangelist Melinda Walker and her Publishing Company Stand In Truth Publications (S.I.T) :

Thank you for the hard work and dedication that was put into publishing my first book. The countless hours and creativity that it took to bring my vision to fruition, thank you. It was a pleasure working with you and I look forward to doing life with you on many more projects. You took what I gave you and made it a reality. I learned that you are a person of their word, very efficient and effective. You are a person of integrity and a person that is passionate about a person's truth being told in a way it will help the next person that may be struggling with similar test and trials in life. I love how you could take a conversation we had and bring life to apart of my life and put it so clearly on paper. I thought that was awesome and wondered how you knew me so well when we have only known each other for a short period of time. You came very highly recommended and I must say, you did not disappoint. Thank you for making my dream into a reality. Now on to our next book. Volume 2. When The Dust Settles.

Special thanks to:

Prophetess Angela Boutwell

Special thanks to Angela Boutwell, an upcoming famous author, who has authored many books and has been very instrumental to many as a co-writer behind the scenes with new writers.

This woman has encouraged and inspired me to author this book. God has blessed her to have her spiritual handprint all over this book. I just want to personally thank you for helping me author this book. You have been very inspirational in my life. In the process of working with you through this, may God continue to bless you and your family. Thank you! Dee

Special thanks to:Author/Administrator/Friend
Barbara White

Special thanks to Barbara White, the author of *They Don't Fall*, and "Fighting With No Tears' wonderful books. Look for her books if you are a book enthusiast.

My childhood school friend, whose idea it was for me to author this book. She pushed me until I started writing. She has been a major help inspiring me and being by my side all the way through this process. Barbara, I could not have done it without you.

I realize that some friends come and go, but some friendships are a lifetime or until death comes.

You have been a big blessing to my life, and you are indeed my friend for life.

Appreciatively

Your Friend,

Dee

~ He Knows My Name ~

To My Beloved Wife,

Barbara

Where would I be without the strong backbone of my Queen? She has held me down, believed in me when no one else did, been my greatest cheerleader, my best friend, my best confidant, and the best woman that God saved just for me.

Baby, this journey… I did not walk it alone; you were right here by my side, and for that I thank you. My gratitude comes right from the deepest part of me: my heart. the spirit of God interconnects us, and you were my gift from the Heavenly Father. The scriptures say, in Proverbs 18:22, "He that finds a wife finds a good thing."

~ He Knows My Name ~

You are my good thing, and I will forever shower you with everything you deserve. I will always be the man you prayed for. You are the best part of me.

You are the love story that everyone desires to write, but only I know the words that should lay upon the paper.

As the love song that reminds me of you "Betcha" by Golly Wow says: "You're the one that I've been waiting for forever and ever will my love for you keep growing' strong, keep growing' strong."

Thank you, baby, for your continued encouragement and patience. I love you more than any words could ever say. Smooches, Love.

Your very own,

Your Husband

~ He Knows My Name ~

Special Thanks to:
Pastor Keith Evans

I met Pastor Evans some years ago. When we first met it was something about our spirits that connected right away. He was there for me when I was going through my darkest hour and my biggest pain dealing with the loss of my daughter and granddaughter. I would give Pastor Evans a call and I would stop by his church and Pastor Evans took time to listen to me and give me words that helped me get through my grieving process. Pastor Evans always found time to be there for me. Pastor Evans was a good listener, and he would share his own experiences with me that I could relate to. What he did was amazing. We would share together, pray together, and talk things out. He was a brother that was always there for me. For that I am eternally grateful. Then I called him a good brother, a listening ear and good counsel. Today I call him Pastor, friend and confident.

Foreword:

Pastor Daryn D. Crenshaw

Dyland Weather has, through this work, positioned the reader in full view of the prophetic process of Spiritual maturation. Before I expound on that, I want to tell you how Dyland and I know each other, as I believe that people share time and space for a reason.

In November 1999, having gone south to secure formal theological training, I returned to the city of my birth, Racine, Wisconsin to pastor full-time. Like Chicago, Racine sits on the shores of Lake Michigan, but unlike Chicago, one of the largest cities in America, Racine's population is less than 100,000 citizens. I was called to this mission field to be a change agent and lead a transformation of the mind for those searching souls I would meet.

I must say, giving all Glory and Honor to God, The Lord's Church grew, and people of all walks of life found solace in the Worship and Works of the Church. I remember preaching in the city at another church in the community, and after the worship experience, a young man shook my hand, looked me in the eye, and said, "Preacher, that's what I needed to hear." It didn't stop there. This young man (Dyland Weather) interviewed me. If he asked me one question, I'm sure he asked me a hundred that night. I was impressed though; he had received God's revelation for his life, and it resonated with him. Interestingly, he also wanted to know the person behind the sermonic exercise. There was no shame in his game. He valued information and hungered for Good, Godly Growth. From this initial encounter and many more like it, Dyland and I have personally traveled throughout this country promoting the gospel and providing physical and financial aid through missionary work. From the humble beginnings in the big city of Chi, all the way to the land-locked city of Racine and all over this country of ours, I witnessed firsthand the spiritual transformation of Brother Dyland, and I believe he has it right – He Knows His Name!

It was Booker T. Washington who said, "Excellence is to do a common thing in an uncommon way." The Apostle Paul talks about the diversity of gifts. The life story, as we are presented within *He Knows My Name* expresses the personal excellence that allows a rose to grow from the concrete and share its beauty with those it encounters. Dyland's life is that rose: a seed sowed, watered, and nurtured by the Hand of God. How else can one explain the level of protection and perseverance it took to make it out of the projects and yet still possess the peace of mind that surpasses all understanding? Brother "D", as he is affectionately known, shares with the reader that he is not perfect, but he strives for perfection as is the biblical mandate by using the gifts God has given him – to transform him first and, secondly, those he encounters on this journey.

To you, the reader, I pray you find in the following pages, life transformation in the life of author, and hope, faith, and love enough to change any situation. Pastor Dr. Daryn D. Crenshaw

Introduction

This book was born in this season of my life because I have realized how good God is while on this mission. From birth, God had His hands on me, and He has covered and protected me even through my adversities.

Spending many months, weeks, days, hours, and minutes even up to this present moment as I write, has been such a rewarding time through heart-wrenching reality, thoughts, tears, laughter, and pain in reflecting back. I am now able to recognize my purpose in life. It is for me to be transparent with all my readers to allow them into my private world of truth.

As you read this book, please read with an open heart and mind, without forming any judgmental thoughts or feelings but knowing that none of us were created perfect. I will be the first to admit I did many wrong things in my life and have paid greatly. The good thing about life is when you recognize you have wronged others as well as yourself, we serve a God that is forgiving, and once we have been forgiven, He throws our sins right into the sea of forgetfulness and holds it not against us as man does. Through my lifelong journey, I have learned to forgive others in the process and hold not one grudge in my heart toward anyone.

Every day is a new day, and I am a new man with all praises going to the Heavenly Father. I do not expect every reader to understand my life or like my flavor, but, man, if not, I will not hold it against you if you do not sip my cup. This may not be your flavor of the day. In the event that you are a connoisseur of good coffee, and you like my flavor, may your taste buds be stimulated to continue to turn the pages.

Being transparent is the best version of me, clean and uncensored. Through my journey as I have walked my path; I am living my best life now. Living, loving, and laughing my way through the steps that my God has personally ordered for me in order for me to reach my destiny. If I reach for the moon and land on the stars, it is still a good day, and it teaches me to never give up because I will, with God's help, reach the moon.

You must know that I give all praise first to my Lord and Savior. He has sustained my life, given me new life, and continues to bless me each and every day that He allows me to live. With him being the captain of my ship, He guides my sails as His wind is beneath my wings.

Sit back, put your feet up, and let us go for the ride together, as we journey through the pages of my life.

~ Chapter 1 ~
The Imagination of the Young

Chicago sits right on Lake Michigan in Illinois and is among one of the largest cities in the United States. Chicago is also referred to as the Windy City or Chi Town. It's known for its famed skyline with skyscrapers such as the Sears and Roebucks Towers, which is now called Willis Tower. This tower, which happens to be 1,451 ft., is the tallest building in Chi Town with 131 floors. Wow! What an elevator ride this is. When you are a child, this seems so gigantic.

Aside from the fact that Chicago is known for so many things and so much more that catches the attention of the residents, visitors, and tourists, Chicago is really no different from any other large city in America.

Chicago has some of the most well-known projects like Robert Taylor, Cabrini Green, and Henry Horner, just to put you up on a few of them. These well-known spots are really referred to by some as the hood and are now being dismantled. Like any other large urban city on the map, the African Americans previously moved from the city to find the suburbs and the feeling that they had arrived. The city was becoming raggedy back in the day, so having a better house in the burbs was thought to be the classier move. Now the White population realized "Wow, the African Americans have all moved out, so let's move back into the inner city." So, now my white brothers and sisters are moving back into prime realty locations like condos on the lake, condos and apartments downtown and closer to everything. Caucasians are moving back into the city as it is being redeveloped for them. Things like this always seems to take a turn in every city across the United States. Then we notice an influx of people flocking to new areas being built, rehabbed, or renovated from storehouses, apartment buildings, and are not limited to new homes being built.

I remember being a young child growing up on the south side of Chicago. I was living in the projects as a kid. Most people know that projects are the low-income housing available for those who have little to no income to properly take care of the family, as I have shared above. Families back in the day sacrificed and found a way to make it. Interesting how things that were setup for our failure have slowly begin to turn themselves around. Families in the hood are slowly picking their bootstraps up and desiring so much more for their family.

Living in the projects, there was always something going on in my neighborhood. Hey, never a dull moment. Often it was like a war zone that was full of violence, guns, drugs, gangs, plenty of women, and sex. As a teenager, it did not get no better than that. You would know this on contact. You could find it all somewhere there, so much that if Ray Charles were living, he would see it, and the brother was a blind man. There was never a dull moment in the projects.

In Chicago, the city that never sleeps, anything could erupt at any given time. It made no difference: in the wee hours of the early morning, noon, evening, or nighttime. Who would even think that bullets would have a time attached to them, am or pm? Neither one, not am or pm. No time at all unless ordered by the hit man. We all knew that bullets fly 24 hours a day, at any given time, and have no name on them.

The violence has gotten so out of hand that babies, infants, toddlers, children, teens, young adults, and even our elderly are being shot down in the streets.

It is sad. Kids cannot play outside free and innocent without some silly goose doing a drive-by on a street or playground full of children. Even kids feel the tension in the streets, and to them it is like being in a prison without cells despite never even experiencing one.

Just thinking back to when we were kids, whenever gun shots would sound off, my mom would yell, "Get down! Get down!" When we would hear the sounds, we would hit the floor. It was like being in Beirut. My mother would be screaming to get away from the windows and get down. We would be on the ground 20-30 minutes at a time, no moving at all until the sounds completely stopped.

As a kid, hearing things like that just put bold fear in me. The fear in my mom's eyes caused me so much pain, yet I had to be strong. I just learned to put on my superman cape, to save the day. Fear was hard to adjust to, but I did, which made me harder.

Can you imagine a mother crying out to protect her children, helpless to what was happening outside of her doors, shielding us from all that was going on just outside our window? So many mothers lost their children, and every mother supported each other more than ever in this season. You dare not ask personal questions; you might just get your head chewed off.

~ He Knows My Name ~

Back in the day, you did not have to wait for the news to travel home to your parents. You would get stopped on contact. If it was not the principal, it was Mr. and Mrs. Beltstrap putting you in line. The village at the time helped raise the children.

What is this world coming to? You cannot even look at someone's kids before the parents are twisting up their faces. No respect by even the toddlers let alone the teenagers. Go figure. Who's going to help get these kids together?

For those of us who have that deep seeded respect and knowledge, we must be the change we want to see. We have to train and educate our culture starting with the families, the children, the schools, and the community. We are failing, and we can grab the tiger by the tail, not letting the tiger chase us.

~ Chapter 2 ~

A Mother's Nightmare

Momma had no clue that one day she would have her own experience with one of her own kids. It was the summer of 1972; we were returning from one of our summers getaway. My dad would always take us to the south to visit family.

Well, we arrived home one day, and we were getting out of our car, and yes, it started by bullets flying everywhere. How scary this was for all of us and just to hear my momma screaming. Mother began to say, "Get down! Get down!" As I looked over to my brother, he was already down on the ground. People were running, trying to escape the bullets; it was awful, and all you could hear was screaming and feet shuffling in the midst of it all.

After a while, the shots stopped. We all slowly started to get up. All except my brother, and my mom ran over to him screaming "My baby is shot! My baby is shot!" My dad dropped to the ground, holding my brother, screaming, "Somebody please call 911! My baby has been shot!"

A neighbor called the ambulance. We knew they would not arrive until the sounds were completely gone. We all waited in silence. The look in my mom's eye was the look of a mother who did not know what to do to help.

She had one son laying on the ground and three other children that stood nearby, looking at her for comfort.

~ He Knows My Name ~

While we waited for the ambulance to come get my brother, we heard that another kid had just been shot right in the next building. So close. That kid was my brother's best friend. Really, we were all like family. Out of the village, more fear rose.

My parents had four children, and my brother Robert was the oldest one of us all. My brother was 11 months older than I, and he was shot at the age of eight. We also had two sisters, Wendy, and Lisa, younger than I. We clung together, and we had to stay with the neighbor until our parents came back to get us. Actually, this is what families did then, a village helping out as they did in the seventies.

That was a terrible tragedy for us to endure at such an early age. I still have faint memories of that today, and I can see it as if it just happened yesterday. I believe my whole family was scared by that. It took a terrible toll on my mother. Can you imagine, seeing your first-born laying helplessly on the ground lifeless and not being able to do anything except hold him?

Although, my brother did survive through the grace of God, the giver of life, he spent the entire summer in the hospital recovering. He had to learn how to walk and talk again, among other things. Again, the grace of God.

I can say that my brother is a miracle. God brought him through this. He recovered 100%, I would say. There were no deficits at all. He went on to be a smart young fella. He became an A student, and he even made the honor roll.

My mother developed a resentment for the projects. In her mind, her baby was hurt badly and would not have been if we did not reside in the projects. This is the same place where my dad worked and made money to take care of his family. My dad was a janitor in the projects and in the very building we lived in.

My mom was very fearful of the projects, a common fear that most mothers shared that has caused her family pain. Momma would often tell my dad, enough is enough. "Get us out of this jungle, please." Indeed, it was a jungle that included being a rat race for families and our neighbors. My dad would tell her, "Just let me save up some more money, and I will get you that dream house you deserve. I promise I will."

Personally, I feel like a mother is an overseer who governs and protects her family. As some may say, she is the mother goose who watches out for her goslings and the father goose.

I was so glad to have positive people in my life like my grandmothers. They saw something in me that I had no clue of. They continued to impart positivity in me, and the download in my mind was taking place when I did not even know it.

All I ever wanted was to be happy, joyous, and free. I always needed to have something or someone to make me feel different. Whether it was alcohol, drugs, sex, or indulging in any substance that made me feel good. Having those things is what I thought I needed to make me feel whole and worthy. We must know that worthiness is a privilege as well as our internal desire to conquer what is satisfying to us.

~ Chapter 3 ~

Lights, Camera, Action

Growing up in my environment…well, it was not common to show any signs of weakness. I had to keep my surviving skills on point. My defense mechanism was always up.

There was no such thing as being transparent, and you could not let your left hand know what your right hand was doing at all. Transparency did not exist in the projects, probably because it was a dog-eat-dog world, and the projects were unique, in their own way. It was like a city within a city. There was a seven mile stretch of buildings. People living seventeen stories high, one hundred and sixty apartments in each building, and people living on top of each other. Never a dull moment. Always something to do.

It was like living on a big stage, and everybody had a part to play, and, boy, did I play my part well. Hey, it was like orchestrating a one man play, and I was the character, the only one listed in the cast line-up, and the director of the play. Yes. Camera, lights, action. When it was time for the Ghetto Oscar Awards, for my many roles, guess who received the largest Oscar, the King of the Streets?

I did not make the situation any better. My mom lived on pins and needles the entire time. I know she was tired of my foolery. I was the mischievous kid, always getting myself into trouble. Man, trouble just followed me all over the place without me asking it to come along.

~ He Knows My Name ~

For the life of me, I just could not understand what was wrong with me. I was a lost kid, full of fear, and I had no sense of direction. I was simply in the lane called lost. When I think back, I was bullied as a child, which did not make me feel good about myself. I remember having to fight on my way to school and fight on my way home from school.

I was this skinny kid with a funny shaped head. I had several nick names. None of them were cool names. Names like Squig and Skillet. All my friends had cool nick names, like Skip, Ray Ray, or Pookie. Not like the cartoon characters I was called, always being the butt of somebody's jokes.

People often made jokes about my last name, always asking what the weather would be like today or if I checked the weather before coming out.

I did whatever I could to fit in. I became a people person, pulling whoever in that would listen. Yet, I still managed to find trouble. My first run in with the cops was when some of my friends and I were playing in the back of the building one day, and we came across a bag. The bag had a gun in it. My friend pulled the gun out, and of course, bullets were in the bag. We had never seen a gun up close and personal. Well, my friend pulled the gun out the bag, and, yes, it was loaded. Suddenly, my friend let one loose in the air, and you can imagine what was next.

The police just happened to be patrolling the area. They heard the shot and started coming toward us. We saw them and started to run. They were faster, and we got caught. At that time, I was 12 years old.

~ He Knows My Name ~

We were taken to jail. My mom and dad were called to come down to the station. I knew this would not be a good look at all. My mom had that disappointed look in her eye. That look that I could not bear to see. I knew she would not be happy about this at all, but trouble was riding my back all the time as a kid. I knew she was disappointed in me.

I got supervision. The judges told me this was a serious charge, and if I were not careful, I would end up returning here or spending the rest of my life in jail or something worse could happen. He asked me to be mindful of the danger in the world. He said I was lucky to get probation this time and not to come back again.

I stayed out of trouble for a while. I really did not know what to think. I had what you might call addictive thinking, addictive behavior, and neither better than the other.

Our family was close. We often spent time with other relatives on the weekends, visiting this side of the family or another side of the family. I did my best to stay focused during visits.

The adults stayed in the grown folk's area while me, my sisters, brother, and cousins had to stay in another area, whether we were outside or inside. The adults had their own space. They gave us respect and made sure we stayed in our place — and space — as children.

However, the older of the kids learned to bartend early on. As a teenager, I learned how to pour drinks and open beer. Me and my cousin had to fetch when called to get whatever they needed. So really, we were their little runners for lack of a better word.

My little mind was being visually imprinted with this behavior at an early age. Who would have ever thought this was being downloaded in my brain? All kids have a curious nature of many things. Why? Because we were still developing mentally.

While fixing drinks and opening beers, I got curious about what the adults got out of this and wondered what it tasted like. I saw relatives just drinking one right after another, so I decided to give it a taste. Wow, my taste buds were turned on to the 10th degree. I liked it, so every time I was called to make a drink, I took a drink. That right there was the beginning of my love for alcohol.

After being talked about, bullied, teased, and losing the little self-esteem I had, drinking took away the fear that I lived with, and then I felt my help coming. It gave me courage, the courage to say or do whatever I felt. I squared my shoulders up and walked with confidence. You know, they say believe what a drunk says cause when you are drunk or been drinking, you will say whatever comes to mind first.

I also found out that I was an entertainer. My mom and aunts were the DJs. They would always call me to dance. Hey, I was Michael Jackson and James Brown at the same time. They would be their favorite choices. They played the songs, and I did a mean impression of whomever they played. I was one of the best imposters around, as we say it "cold." After I would finish dancing, I would get money, and I thought, "Wow." It was being formulated in my mind at an early age:

dance and act, and they would show me the money. Now, how cool is that for a pip squeak?

The drinking gave me courage, and dancing started me clocking dollars at an early age. It was like commanding the dollars to come to me. This was the life, one that I liked. Commanding the money $$$$.

~ Chapter 4 ~

Through the Eyes of Others

The older I became and the bigger my taste buds got, the greater challenges came for making money to drink, and not soon after that, drugs followed. The reckless behavior began, so let the good times roll.

It is funny how others seem to speak over your life by sharing their points of views, even when not asked. Opinions are like butt holes, we all have only one. I was often told from friends and relatives that I would end up dead or locked up. I was told I would never amount to anything. That is negativity being implanted into the ears of the listener. Those words rested in my mind for years to come, and I started to believe those words to be true.

Just to take notes, adults should never speak these things to children or teens. It is like speaking a curse over that person's life. You should always speak positivity into the ears of the children, to build them up before the world tries to tear them down.

As a result of that, I often got in trouble. I remember my dad would send me to San Antonio, Texas to stay with his mother during the summer months. Perhaps he thought I was getting away from the roughness of the Chi. He sent me there to keep me out of trouble and to keep me safe.

As I think about my sweet grandmothers, they were the ones who actually spoke life into me. Positivity, yes, I got from both and my parents as well.

~ He Knows My Name ~

Whenever I went to my grandmother's house, I felt like the fresh prince of Bellaire. My demeanor had developed into this cool cat. Yes, I had game and plenty of it by now.

I got close to my grandmother, and our relationship grew during my time with her. She was loving, kind, and I knew who loved me. She took me under her wings and nurtured me like a grandparent should do. She told me never to believe the things of the world, not to trust negativity. She always told me that one day I would make a difference in the world and that I will become somebody one day.

Wow, when I think of this today, my grandmother was speaking over my life. Those tender words she spoke definitely resonated in my mind. My grandmother spoke faith, and I did not even realize what faith was. The scriptures say, in Hebrews 11:1, "Now faith is the substance of things hoped for and the evidence of things not seen."

My mom's mother lived in Chicago. She also was a very kind and sweet grandmother. I had two wonderful grandmothers. Me and my Chicago grandmother shared the same birthday: June 5th. We had lots in common. It was a Gemini thang. It was funny how she often told me the same thing that my Texas grandmother told me about myself. I loved my grandmothers, both of them. My grandmothers both reminded me of my worth, and that gave me hope.

There's something about grandmothers that make them special. When they are gone, wow, cannot get another one, might I share. My grannies were cool in their own way.

Because of the positivity being given to me, it caused me to think about who I was really going to become.

~ Chapter 5 ~

"My Downfall"

Lust of The Eye

Lust of The Flesh

Pride of Life

Thinking back, I always had dreams of becoming an entrepreneur. You see, I had to bring in some income to help support my lifestyle. This was easy to do because I saw my father do it. I learned how to bring in many streams of income.

I loved clothes. Clothes were my thing, as well as cars and women. I got that from my dad. My dad was a hardworking man/player. I would often catch my dad with several different women behind my mom's back.

On the other hand, he was a hardworking man that took care of his family. He gave us everything we needed, even everything we wanted and then some.

We had a beautiful apartment on the fourth floor, in one of the red brick buildings. Mom did her thing when it came to decorating our home. We, as children coming up, learned from both of our parents. As far as Mom and Dad, they both loved wonderful things. This is really where my flavor for wonderful things came from. Some people around me were not as fortunate to have what we were given.

~ He Knows My Name ~

As kids, we all had nice clothes and shoes. We also ate very well. We had the finer things in life. For living in the projects, we lived the life.

Some of my friends did not have what we had, so my dad would treat them as if they were his own kids. My dad would never turn any of my friends away. Never turned a deaf ear to them. My dad was cool like that.

Wow, I remember some of my friends did not have a Merry Christmas, so my dad would always get extra toys so we could share with them.

Whoever was there got to open toys from under the tree, so we could all enjoy the gifts together at Christmas time. There were other holidays that we shared with my friends as well, like the 4th of July, Thanksgiving, Labor Day, Easter, and Memorial Day. Having my friends over was welcomed by all of us. My friends were like family to all of us. No one was treated any different by my mother and father.

I remember getting our first colored tv. We was the first in our neighborhood. My friends were all fascinated. They would say, "You guys are living ghetto fabulous." I was always eager to look out for my friends. I remember my dad telling me I was more of a friend to my friends than they were to me. I now realize that was very true based on the tender heart I had. I was very sensitive to their needs because of my kind heart. It took me a while to understand what my dad was really saying to his son. Yes, it was true: fathers seem to always know best.

I did not know if I was people pleasing or just trying to fit in. However, I believe in trusting and treating people right.

~ He Knows My Name ~

To do the right thing even if wrong showed up. Wrong
always had a way of finding me, even in the midst of my
greatness and goodness. Those were the values my mom put
into all of us. Oh, how sweet my mom was.

We were her four children: two boys and two girls. My
brother was always the brain of the family. My two younger
sisters, Lisa, and Wendy, were the jewels of the family. It was
the brothers' job to protect them. So, early in life we
developed a nature to watch over our sisters. We had a great
upbringing.

We traveled. We had more than most families. We
prayed together. We ate together as a family, and we also
went through our struggles together. What happened in
apartment 408 stayed in apartment 408. We were taught to be
private by not airing out our business.

Girls. Wow! I always had a liking for girls. One day, I
was roaming through my dad's dresser drawer, and I ran
across a playboy magazine. Oh, yeah, that was the day I saw
my first naked woman. A body in full view. Right away it got
me excited. It was if I had experienced this before. Her
pictures were exciting, and it made the drive for sexuality
come alive.

My sister had this friend that would come over and
stay for a sleepover. I knew her friend had a liking for me. I
did not feel the same for her as she felt for me, but she was a
girl.

My attraction was sexual only. I would sneak her into
my bedroom at night. We would bump and grind. One night
it happened: we went from kissing and grinding right into the

real thing. I do not think either one of us knew just what to do, but we went all the way without protected sex.

I was seventeen, and she was sixteen. I thought, *Wow, we both broke our virginity tonight*. It was a night I will never forget.

I never thought that a child would have come from that night, until the day my sister came and told me that her friend was pregnant, and I was the father. I said, "Oh, no. Not me. Your friend is just trying to put her hook in me." I said, "I don't make babies."

I remember when she gave birth, the baby came out looking just like me. She was the spitting image of me. Like a fool, I was still in denial.

We ended up in child support court. The court officer was sitting right next to the baby's mother. He looked over at me and looked at the baby. He then said, "Are you really going to stand in front of the judge and deny this baby?"

I put my head down.

Deep down inside I knew she was mine. I took a deep breath and said to the officer, "No, I am not. This case is closed. She is my baby. I am her father. Yeah, she is my baby." That was the day I accepted my baby girl, Donysha . I said, "She is my baby."

I really was not ready for this thing called fatherhood. When you ask yourself, who is really ready? When you are in your teens, you never really plan for the inevitable if you are doing the do. I guess I thought I was in the prime of my player-hood. I was in the prime of being a teenager. I was still in high school.

My dad had just bought me a Cadillac, and I was that fly guy in high school. It was a 1974 coupe Deville, two years old. Brother, you could not tell me nothing. You see I had it all, or so I thought at the time.

I had this side hustle in the hood. I had a weed business, and it was going well. I was the man in school. Oh, yeah. The girls were all paying attention, and they were everywhere. My ego was as big as New York City. Life was so good I started spending more time in my Cadillac than I did at school. Go figure.

So, me and my boys started this organization called the business organization. My right hand man was Calvin, and right next to him was Lil Tone. Some called us the three Amigos. None of us really cared for that name.

Where there was one of us, there were all three of us, inseparable. We made a fashion statement to die for. We was always suited and booted from head to toe. We always kept brief cases in our right hands, and it was always full of money. We had mad respect from everybody in our neighborhood. We had an image to uphold and seeing us was like watching *The Mack*. We all know who the Mack was, right?

I decided that school was not for me. My guys stayed in and completed high school. I reached 11th grade and said, "Hey, this is not my style. I got bigger and better on the bricks." So, I dropped out. How smart was that? I am still trying to figure out this thing called life

~ He Knows My Name ~

My mom was not happy with that at all. She showed that disappointed look, but I felt I knew best. My dad made several attempts to take the car away. My ego once again got in the way and grew bigger and bigger. I was at a point where you could not tell me nothing. I knew everything already; I was that man. I had finally arrived. People would have to take their foot and give me a push to get through the doors.

I was no longer dating girls my age; they were not on my level. I started dating older women or older girls. At that time, they were called vets. They loved taking care of this young, fly brother. I had a woman in every building. Once again, *The Mack*, just think about it.

I would pull up in the neighborhood with that long Cadillac, jump out dressed in the flyest threads. Now my walk was so distinguished you could tell who I was a mile away, even in the dark.

I always had a pocket full of money because it was coming in from all over the city. My dad sat me down one day and said, "Hey, son, you are moving a little too fast. I am very much concerned about you. Your name is flowing throughout this town more than I care to hear." My dad said, "Listen to this: you have got to slow it down." My dad shared he had found me a job.

My first thought was *I do not want a job*, but clearly, I knew my dad was right. I said, "Okay. You are right again, Dad."

My dad set me up with a job with his company. I knew I never had a legit job, and my hustle was flowing smooth.

~ He Knows My Name ~

My dad kept his promise to my mom. He moved her out of the projects into that dream home.

I decided to remain at the apartment. The rent was free because my dad worked there, so why not? I took over the apartment and was now living as a bachelor in my own pad.

~ Chapter 6 ~

Coming to the End of Myself

After a while, I moved my daughter and her mother in with me. I wanted us to be a family. I tried to do the best I could to maintain this family life.

Another girl was pregnant and about to have my second baby.

Okay, let me just inform you that my first daughter's mom and I were never in a relationship. We had a sexual relationship, and she got pregnant. This all came about from her spending the night with my sister, and we did it, and she got pregnant.

Now when my second child was born, this was a little different story. Her mother was a quiet girl who went to a catholic school and very well kept. She was one of the prettiest girls in our neighborhood. I actually started seeing her from a bet with my boy, Cal. I said one day, "Hey, I bet I can pull her. I think I have the right game for her." He took the bet, and it was on. Of course, I won.

There were a lot of guys in the hood who wanted her. But I got her. She accepted my invitation to go out. I put my best game down and got her. We got into it soon after we started to date.

I do not know why, but it was not long after we had started dating that she got pregnant. I could produce fast. Making babies was easy for me.

~ He Knows My Name ~

I did not fight this birth. I had learned my lesson. I did not try to deny this baby. I knew better.

I remember the summer of 1984. I went to New York. I left the bachelor pad with my sister. I told her to watch it while I was in New York on a business trip.

I arrived back in two months to find a pregnant girl in my apartment. Who just happened to be my second baby momma. I mean, she was all moved in. I asked, "What's the deal here?" She said her mom found out she was pregnant and told her she had to go. And my sister took her in. I was not ready for that because the pad was about to get jumping, but she was my baby's momma. I guess it was time to give up the bachelor pad and time to raise my kids.

Wow, what a change from what I was used to. I did my best to make a happy and comfortable place for us all.

Well, I was not cut out for being a stay at home dad. . I had to get my hustle back on. That is what I knew, and that is where I felt comfortable. I was a player. That's what I did.

My daughter's mother found out that I was seeing other women. She even got ahold of them. They told her they were in a relationship with me. I could not lie my way out of this. She had enough of me.

One summer day, I arrived back home from one of my business trips, and my daughter's mother had packed up and moved out and took half of everything that was in my apartment. I was shocked when I opened the door to a half empty apartment. I stood there for a moment before I turned on the lights, and when I did, things became clear: she was gone. I soon found out that she was not far. She had moved a few blocks down from me.

Wow! This so-called playa was hurt badly by this. What could I do? I moved on. I stepped up my hustle game, trying to forget what had just happened. I started to travel more and started meeting different women.

I began to hook up with other fellas from the neighborhood. These guys were known as Cannons. Cannon is a name for professional pick pockets. They taught me the game. I was always eager about making more money. Selling dope was not enough for me right now. There was a void in my life, and I was chasing it.

I got involved with the Cannons. We went to different events all over the city, like baseball games, playing the subways...anywhere we could find a lot of people was the best place to pick pockets. I would even hop on train, going back and forth, making it happen.

I became what we called a writer (forging signatures). I was pretty good at it. I started to travel from city to city writing. I went across the country to professional events because the stakes were better. I went wherever the money was: super bowls, big fights, baseball games, all the elite events.

Eventually, I got tired of writing and pick pocketing, so I hooked up with one of the doctors in the neighborhood. He was a smart young man; he did things more upscale. He was a credit card player, so I moved on and moved up to the big league. Money was good. Mind you, I had to be under the influence to perform because my courage was incredible during that time.

Soon, I became my own best drug customer, making my need to play the credit cards more intense. I joined a few other brothers, going on the road, playing the credit card scheme.

I ended up in Memphis, catching my first case in forgery. I must have written over $73,000.00 from one card. I kept going and going with this one card until the Feds caught up with us.

I was coming off of a big shopping spree, trying to buy some cameras. We were leaving the mall, walking to the car and an undercover car rolled up on us. We had no idea they had been following us from the moment we made it to town. Once we spotted them, we scattered. I turned and went back in the store as if I had to get one last thing. I got greedy.

They came down on me. I was arrested. I had to go before a judge, who sentenced me to a year and a day in a federal prison. I was charged with four counts of forgery. I did that time in Memphis.

After that, I got out and hooked up with this young lady. She was a high yellow girl, a red bone. This girl was gorgeous, and fine as wine. I fell for her real fast and real hard. She understood me and what I was about. We had a lot in common. She had that instinct to hustle in her. She was also a writer. We were chasing the same things. Money and our next high. Our attraction for each other was the same. We were a match made in heaven. Well, that is what I told myself.

~ He Knows My Name ~

We began to work together, hustling. We was getting that paper, baby. I was in love with her, and I believed she felt the same for me.

Here it is 1988. We pulled off a stain with some dope dealers. We hit them up for a huge amount. We checked into a hotel downtown and smoked our brains out. We went through a lot of money that weekend; we still had a lot of money left. We could not go back to the place where it took place. The guys had put out a manhunt for us. We searched for a new location.

Finally, she said, "I have the perfect spot for us. My brother lives up in Wisconsin. I know he will let us crash with him until we figure out our next move." She gave him a call. He gave us the green light, and we were on our way. I had never been to the city before, so it was a new beginning for me.

When we got there, we knocked on the door for a while, but there was no answer. After a while, the landlord came out and asked who we were looking for, and when we told her, she stated, "You are a day short." She told us the police had just picked him up the previous day.

Immediately our hustle instincts kicked in. We got the landlord to allow us to stay and take over his rent until he was released.

Well, he never came back. He had been charged.

We still had a large amount of dope on us, and we had to stay low, even in this small town. Here we are living in

~ He Knows My Name ~

Racine, neither one of us knew anyone. We were full blown in our addiction . We decided to make this our home.

We became instant drug dealers. Getting the word around did not take long. About two months passed. Our families had no idea where we were. They did not know if we were dead or alive. One day, I knew that it was time to check in, so I called my dad to let him know where I was. Not surprised, he told me he had gotten word people were looking for me, and he was very concerned about me. He told me he was glad I called; however, he let me have it. He told me just how he felt about how I was handling my life.

The dope and money were gone, and my lady was now dope sick. She needed heroin. She decided to take a trip to the city but thought that it would be safer to go alone, just in case people were still looking for us. I did not want her to go alone, but I had no choice. Our lives were at risk. She went to Chicago one weekend alone, looking for help.

I waited for her to come back. While I waited, I had to get back on my hustle here in Wisconsin. Days passed. I became worried about her. I had no way of finding out if she was still safe or not. I went back to Chicago to try and find her. I searched high and low but never found her, so I went back to Wisconsin and laid low.

After some time had passed I ran into this guy I knew and asked had he seen her and he told me she had died. This was a hard pill to sallow. I was in shock. I had to get a fix for myself, so once again, I fell back to my old ways and back into the old habit of doing crime. I landed in and out of jail for a period of time.

~ He Knows My Name ~

I kept telling myself, *Something has got to change. I cannot keep living like this. I am killing myself slowly.* I did not know what to do. I did not know what was happening. It was as if I was out of my body. I knew I needed a change, but I did not how to get it. I did not have a clue as to what to do or where to go.

I really did not understand what was going on in my life. Here I am in a town with no family, no friends. My life was disappearing fast.

I ran into a few guys I had met here. We became good with hanging out with each other. They were different from me. All they did was drink a few beers, nothing else. One of them helped me out and told me about a available job where he worked.

I decided to make this place home. I needed a change, and I would do that here. This town was slow enough for me to catch up and start over. It reminds me of Mayberry. Adjusting was a challenge, but I needed a change.

After a while, I went back to visit Chicago. I think I stayed too long. I first went to my mother' house, sleeping in her basement. Nobody was looking for me. I often wondered how that bill was settled. I will never know.

It was not long after being there until I ran into Gail, a girl I had dated back in the day. This was not a good choice, but I moved into her house, sleeping in her basement. It was not good because we were both full blown into our addiction.

Here I go again, I often thought. *This is not who I am. I have to get out of this.*

~ He Knows My Name ~

My birthday was coming, and two of my drinking buddies came up from Wisconsin. I hung out with them. I told them of my situation, and they invited me back to stay with them. Of course, I went because I wanted better. Chicago was not the town for me. I finally figured that part out. I left and said, "Lord, I have to try. I have to try."

I went back and got an impressive job with the intent to do better. I stopped drinking, stopped doing drugs. I was now six months clean. It felt so good. I kept telling myself, "I am healed." I was doing great.

Another six months passed, and low and behold, I picked up both the drugs and the drinking. The urge just hit me, and I could not resist. I fell hard right back into a slump. I was now at rock bottom and did not know if I would ever look up again.

I ran to the first sign of a 12-step program. I needed help. I saw my life drifting away.

Things started looking up for me. were. I was working this program. I now had a few months under my belt. I felt somewhat better about myself. was. I had a great sponsor; he was doing an excellent job helping me stay sober.

I landed another job. I met another lady. We started a relationship. At this point, I am feeling good about myself. My spiritual life was growing. I was attending church more often, getting involved in the service. Yea, things were looking up.

I believe I got too relaxed. I stepped away from the 12-step program and started spending more time in service. I did not realize that I needed the program to continue my service in church. I felt as if I turned my back on the program. You know, as if I did not need it anymore. It was as if I had this thing in the bag.

Life was good being sober. I felt so good about where I was that I started visiting the old places, preaching to the old crew about how I felt. I would even tell them they needed to get their lives together.

One of the guys from the program saw me and told me he did not think me visiting those places so soon was a clever idea. Hitting spots that you hung out in was not the answer right now.

We have this saying in the recovery game. "If you sit in the barber shop long enough, you will get a haircut." I asked him why he would say that. He replied if you keep visiting them you will become a part of them. I said, "Man, I will never go back to that life again."

That drug demon is always working. One day, I visited the guys, and before I knew it, I ordered a beer. That is all it took. I was back, right back in full force right where I was before. Two days after that I was in a crack house.

I realized at that point that I had a disease. It's called Alcoholism. No matter how long you stay away, you do not start over; you just pick up where you left off, and it goes deeper from there.

Once again, I plunged downhill, skating fast. I remember going on a 30-day binge. Moving from one crack house to another, from one liquor store to another. My disease got me and took control. It had my mind; it was truly calling me.

I walked into my mother's house one night. Everybody stopped, turned, and looked at me. They had not seen me for forty-five days; I was just missing. I showed up looking just like I felt: like something from Hell. I saw disgrace on all their faces.

I could not say a word just walked past them all and headed for the bedroom. I fell on the bed. I believe I slept for three days, only getting up to go to the bathroom. I was too ashamed to face my family, so I stayed in my room. I was worn out, beat down. My body was numb. It was a Sunday evening, and I just laid there.

Suddenly I heard a voice. It said, "Son, I'm here with you."

I looked around. I could not see a face. I could only hear Him. I started to panic. I looked from corner to corner; I could not find where the voice was coming from. I asked, "Who are you?" I heard nothing.

Then He kept calling my name. "Dyland. Dyland." He knew my name. Again, he said, "I am with you always. I will never leave you. Put your trust in me and only me. Remember my word. I will never leave nor will I ever forsake you."

I could then feel His presence. He was so close to me I felt a breath of fresh air blow against my skin. I began to cry. I then felt His arms wrap around me. I felt Him pick me up and put me in His lap. He rocked me, telling me, "Son, it is going to be alright. Go on now. Pick up your bed and go."

~ He Knows My Name ~

I cried out, "Lord, is that you? Give me a sign."

Again, the voice said, "Pick up your bed and go!"

I knew God knew my name.

~Chapter 7 ~

Coming Full Circle

Here I am at a point of no return. Afraid to look down the street too far. I did not want to be in a hurry. I did not want to stumble. I could not afford to fall again. My life had taken too many hard trips, and I needed stability. I needed balance.

At this point, I did not know who I was. I was spiritually bankrupt, financially bankrupt, and surely mentally bankrupt. I had no idea who I was as a man. I was walking around with no spirit. I was lost. I had no soul. I declared I had to make a change, a profound change. Giving up was not an option.

I remember when I was out roaming the streets, going from one dope house to another chasing down hits. I did not want that for myself anymore.

One night, I ran into another brother I used to get high with. I had not seen him in a long time. He had a refreshing look about him, a fresh look I had never seen on him before. He looked so clean and revived.

I yelled out to him, "Hey, brother, what's going on with you?" Usually when you did not see someone from the hood in awhile, they were either dead or in jail.

He turned and said, "Hey, man, how are you doing? I don't live that life anymore. I cleaned up my act. I joined a program. After being released, I've been clean a few years now."

I felt so ashamed standing there, looking at him. I asked him, "Do you think that program can help me?"

He said, "Sure, man. This program is for all of us. If you want it. But you have to stay focused and be ready to surrender yourself." He asked me, "Are you sick and tired of being sick and tired, D?

I said, "Yes, I am, man. I'm sick and tired of being sick and tired."

He said, "Here is my number. If you are serious, give me a call, and I'll come by and pick you up and take you to a meeting."

The very next morning, when I woke up, I looked over at the table next to me, and my guy's card was sitting there. I picked it up and called him. I had no time to waste. It was now that I needed to start the rest of my life.

When he answered I said, "Man, I believe I am ready. Can you come get me?" Soon after we hung up, he arrived and took me to my first honest meeting. He had no idea he helped put my life on track.

I did not know what to expect when I got there. A group of people just like me sat in a room. We all were in recovery. They began to share their story. The first day I simply sat and listened. I did not know what to say or how much to share. I had to get a feel of how to handle my feelings.

~ He Knows My Name ~

I told my buddy that this program was interesting. I asked what I had to do to join. He said, "We have no fees or dues. The only requirement is that you have to desire to stay clean."

I said, "I am ready. Sign me up."

I began enjoying the recovery process. I loved the fellowship I was in. I got closer to the people that sat around the table. I made meetings regularly because, in my heart, I knew people were placed in my life for a reason. They got to know me, and I got to know them.

When I shared my experience, I shared strength. Some of the things I battled with in my addition and things I suffered with now, being clean. They also shared with me, letting me know I was not alone. We were in it together. If we started drowning, we came together like we were saving the titanic, on board to rescue, throwing a raft or a lifesaver. At that point, when there are two men in the water trying to save one of their own, it does not matter if you were the richest or the poorest man drowning, you become equal.

That is what this fellowship is all about to all of us. I have a sponsor in the program. This guy went through the steps. He went through the whole deal: practicing the steps, spiritual principles. He guided me through the process. His name is James. I love this guy; he knows me better than I know myself. I will forever be grateful to him. I love going to the many functions we have. Experiencing good times without being under the influence. I never thought I could experience or enjoy a clean life. Enjoying picnics that were a blast. We shared weddings, funerals, and so many other events. We bonded together, always being there for each other. I am very grateful for this fellowship.

I cheated. I robbed. I took whatever I wanted, whenever I wanted whether I needed it or not. I lived as a menace to society. I did all of this. I knew it was time I came full circle. I knew I had to be strong and do what was necessary to be free from that demon controlling my life. I wanted out, and I wanted to be free to live a healthy, normal life. It was time I became what I was purposed to be.

God spoke to me again. This time I recognized His voice. He said, "Son, I want you to be a part of a mighty ministry. I want you to be a part of training, just like my Disciples. I want you to go throughout the world helping others, telling them your story." I said Lord, send me I will go!

One thing is for sure. If you walk in the light, your light will surely shine. As long as you are in the will of God. People will notice a difference in you, like my mom and dad. My mom is so proud of me living this brand-new life. Every time she sees me tears roll down her face. She will give me a big hug and say, "Son, I am so proud of you. You are my big baby."

On the other hand, my dad shows his emotions differently. With him, I feel like the prodigal son. Our father and son relationship is a close-knit one. Fathers do not want their son to see them all in tears and emotional, but I could see it in his eyes: how proud he was of me.

~ He Knows My Name ~

I remember a time my dad and I were having a conversation over the phone. We had started talking daily. At the end of our talk I said, "Dad, I love you."

My dad said, "Son, I love you too."

I almost dropped the phone. That was the first time I ever heard my dad say I love you. Do not get me wrong. I knew he loved me; his actions told me always. I always felt his love but hearing him say it was awesome.

When I looked at my parents and my siblings, they gave me the nod of gratitude, saying, "Yes! Keep up the excellent work." That made me feel more willing to walk in the victory of the Lord. Hearing good things from your family is an awesome feeling. Being encouraged knowing all the hell I put them through, all the sleepless nights they faced because of me....

My mom used to pace the floors at night, wondering when her son would come home or if he would come home safe and sound. This makes me more eager to walk in my calling.

Today I am free, and so are the people around me. If nothing else, we are at peace. What a glorious thing. Hallelujah and amen.

I started this organization called "A New Vision For Kids."

I worked with the inner-city kids. We had meetings about outreach. We took them camping, staying in touch with schools, helping where we could. I had mentors to come in and share their stories to help keep the kids on track.

~ He Knows My Name ~

I wanted to give them hope and allow them to dream out of the box, staying positive no matter what walk of life they came from. Anything is possible if you keep your mind on the Lord. Telling them that one day you will be somebody if you do not give in and never give up.

I remember taking the kids on a camping trip. A group of us got about one hundred kids to go. They were all kids at risk, but we had to give them an experience of a lifetime. This was an amazing trip, seeing their eyes light up, being so happy to be there. It was most of the kids' first time going on a camping trip. It was a joy and so rewarding seeing them with fishing rods in their hands. They were so excited. This trip gave them a sense of belonging. We had speakers and mentors that showed up to speak to the kids. It was a beautiful sight. I kept this up. Kids are very important to me. I had plenty of opportunities to share my own life story while praying it would encourage them. I became very busy indeed, and I loved it.

I enjoyed doing this work. I knew it was time to speak out and make a difference. I knew God had changed my life, and in order for me to keep what I had, I had to give it away. I started to go out to visit different schools, sharing my story. With strength and hope, I prayed that if I could help at least one of them then my job was not in vain.

Be it one or many, I had to capture him or them. I wanted to reach out to those who were up and coming, knowing all I had to do was share my story, and my story would keep a kid on the straight path. I knew who I was talking to while I was speaking. I could see the gleam in their eye. My story caught him right in the thought of getting ready to slip, and I would go hard, hard enough to catch him and put a stop to that devil trying to steal another mind. I knew my testimony would someday touch someone if I just had the opportunity to tell the children my story. They would hear how things used to be and how they are today. It is all clear. I now see my purpose. Knowing that God has work for me to do. I understand that my struggle is my purpose.

~ Chapter 8 ~

My Saving Grace

It was August 2003, and I was currently seven months sober. I decided to take a walk on the beach. I walked toward the band shell along North beach. I found a nice spot to just hang out and enjoy the music. The shell had local bands come and play for anyone on the beach. I noticed a young lady sitting at the concession stand, enjoying the music with a friend girl. I was immediately drawn to her. My eyes caught her at first glimpse.

I kept my eyes locked on her until she noticed me. Finally, she saw me, and I knew that it was now or never. I did not want to miss the opportunity to meet her. I had to come up with a game plan. She was a beautiful, sophisticated looking young lady. We kept making eye contact, and a smile here and there, from afar. I had to fix that, so I walked over to them. I said, "Hello, ladies." They both responded. After walking closer, I realized I knew the friend girl she was with, so I spoke and asked them if I could join them. They said yes. I walked over and sat next to the lady I had my eyes on.

I introduced myself, and she did the same. We started talking from there, getting acquainted. I asked if I could get them something to drink. They accepted. We talked for some time, and after a while, they started gathering their things to leave. I could not let her get away without giving her my number. I found an old card in my pocket, and I wrote my number on the back of it and asked her to give me a call.

~ He Knows My Name ~

The young lady started to walk toward the bus stop. I walked and got in my car, and I noticed she was still waiting on the bus. I drove over and asked if I could drop her off. She said, "Sure." I asked if it would be okay if I made a quick stop by the grocery store on the way, and she said, "No problem."

I went in the store and got the things I needed. When I got back to the car, I asked her if she had dinner plans. She had no plans, so I asked her to have dinner with me. She agreed. There was something special about this young lady. I could not put a price tag on it, but I knew I liked the way she made me feel. She amused me. It felt like déjà vu, as if we had met before or I already knew her.

For dinner, I made macaroni and cheese, pork chops, and some vegetables. We sat and talked while eating. After dinner, we watched some TV. I got up to go the bathroom. When I got back; she had fallen asleep on my couch. I could not bring myself to wake her, so I spread a blanket over her and let her sleep.

The next morning when, at 6 am, I got up to prepare for work, she was still sleeping. I did not wake her. I got ready for work, and then I walked over to her and gently shook her. She jumped up and said, "What time is it?" She apologized for falling asleep.

I smiled and said, "Don't worry about it." I told her I would drop her off on my way to work.

At work, this lady was heavy on my mind. While thinking about her, a different feeling took over my emotions. Wow, a feeling that I enjoyed. It was pleasant. I can say that I felt her in my spirit all day long. This lady consumed my thoughts, a feeling I welcomed.

I got home later that day, and I still had her on my mind. Not long after I got home, my phone rang, and it was her. She apologized again for falling asleep. We both laughed it off. I told her she looked so peaceful lying there that I could not bring myself to wake her up. I asked her if she wanted to take in a movie with me, and she said yes. We spent that evening enjoying the movie, and afterwards, we talked, getting to know more about each other.

We began to see more of each other. That is where our relationship began. I enjoyed getting to know her, and she kept accepting my date requests, so it was on. I did not think I was ready for a committed relationship. I had just gotten out of a long relationship, and my guards were up.

She would call every day just to see how I was doing. I found myself waiting and looking forward to hearing from her.

I spoke to one of my friends about how much time she and I were spending together. I told him, "I think it is getting heavy, man. I think she is trying to hook a brother up. I do not know if I am ready for a committed relationship at this time."

He said, "Hey, man, didn't you tell me just last month that you had asked God to place someone in your life? Well, she might be the one God has sent for you.

I answered, "I have been praying for someone special. She might truly be the one. I have this feeling inside I just cannot explain regarding her. I just cannot shake." I thought,

~ He Knows My Name ~

This is the woman for me. She is the one. Four months later we became engaged.

I sat her down and told her everything about my low down and dirty past. I did not hold anything back. I told her about the good, the bad, and the not-so-pretty. We were sitting in my kitchen, sharing life stories. I did not want her to hear about me from anybody other than me, so I laid everything on the table. She listened as I spoke.

After I was done, she said, "I am not concerned about who you used to be. I am only concerned with who you want to be. I am willing to stand by your side and support you on your journey." That moment was the first time I had ever felt wanted. I felt needed. I felt whole.

That night after we had an enjoyable conversation, I had to take her home. She was living with her brother, sleeping on his couch. After dropping her off, I returned home, and I began to talk with God. I said, "Lord, here I am in this apartment alone. I felt complete whenever she was with me." I said, "Lord what shall I do?" The Lord answered and said get up. It was time to bring her home.

I picked up the phone and called her. When she answered, I asked, "What you are doing?"

She said, "Preparing for bed, thinking about you."

I said, "Sweetheart, do me a favor. Get up. Pack your belongings. I am bringing you home.

She said, "What do you mean?"

~ He Knows My Name ~

I said, "I'm bringing you home. I'm on my way. I'll be there in ten minutes." The phone went silent. It was if I could hear tears falling on the other end of the phone. I headed straight to my truck and proceeded to go get her.

When I arrived, I pulled right up to the front door. There she was, waiting patiently. I will never forget how she came over to me and whispered in my ear. "I have been waiting on this moment."

I said, "So have I."

We put her things in the truck, and it was packed to the top, and we headed home. When we got back to the apartment, I wanted to pick her up and carry her across the threshold. I said, "Honey, you are home."

God spoke to me, and I was being obedient. He made things clear to me. He told me that she was the God-given woman for my life. I shared that with her. I declared she was mine.

While dating, I always introduced her as my friend. One evening, we met up with a friend of mine and his wife. I introduced her as my friend, and she smiled and said hello.

As soon as she got the chance, she pulled me aside and said, "We have been together for some time now. We are living together, and I am more than your friend. We crossed that line some time ago. I need for you to decide who I am to you because now I deserve a title."

From that point on, I introduced her to everybody as Barbara, my woman. She was not having that friend thing anymore. I realized she had too much class for that, and I respected her for who she was to me.

We were about four months into our relationship. We had just finished making love one night, and I said to her, "I believe you are my wife."

She looked at me and said, "I believe you are my husband."

At that very moment, I got down on my knees and asked for her hand in marriage. I proposed to her, and she said yes.

She looked at me and said, "Okay. When would you like to do this?"

At this time, it was early winter, and I said, "Let's plan for February 14th."

She agreed that was a good date, and we were set for Valentine's Day. We did our best to live righteous; however, that was hard for us. We were in love and wanted to express our feelings for each other without fear. We knew about fornication, and we wanted to do the right thing before the Lord.

I said to her, "I can't wait until February, sweetheart. Let's get up in the morning and go get our license."

"Okay. Let's do just that."

When we got up the next morning, we went to the courthouse and got our marriage license. We asked the clerk how long did we have to wait until we got married? She said the process takes about 3 weeks, and when it is complete, you can go get married.

We went to our Pastor and asked her to perform the ceremony. She agreed. However, she said we had to complete marriage counseling first.

During one of our sessions, I asked, "Do you think it is too soon for us to get married?"

She asked, "What do you think? Who is before you? If it is God, then that is all you need."

At the time, I was making about $7.50 an hour. We paid the Pastor $30.00, and the congregation got together and did all the decorating and cooking. My family, friends, and church came together and turned this into the most beautiful wedding ever. I am not saying this because it was mine. It was truly very beautiful indeed.

We did not go on a honeymoon right off. We had to save a little more. We did, sometime later, manage to save up enough. I wanted to take my bride to visit my grandmother in San Antonio, Texas.

As soon as my grandmother laid eyes on my wife, she fell in love with her. My grandmother said, "She reminds me of your mother." That is so true. My wife has a lot of my mother's qualities.

~ Chapter 9 ~

He Made Known His Ways to Me

When we returned home from our visit with my grandmother, we got a phone call from my sister, saying my mother had a stroke. We had to rush to her bedside.

While we were waiting, the doctor came out and asked, "Which one of you is P.O.A.?"

We just all looked at each other. I did not think I was the one to make decisions. I did not think I was qualified. I am so glad I did not have to make that decision. My mother lived.

I reflect back, and I can still see the look in my mother's eyes when I dropped out of high school. She gave me the look of disappointment. After this near-death experience, I knew it was time I made my mother proud. After disappointing her so badly, I have to figure out this thing called life.

One of the things I always wanted to do was to start a mentor's group. I wanted to work with the youth. I have a passion for helping kids. Whether they are in a home with one parent or both parents, I believe I have something to share with them. Getting involved with them helps me be a better father/grandfather.

There was so much for me to learn. I had to learn to be a brother, a son, a co-worker, a neighbor, a good relative. These were all major lessons on my to-do list. At one time, I thought I had all these things in the bag. It turned out that I did not have a clue. I had to go through each of these in order to move forward. What I believed was totally false. I accepted each lesson like a man.

I started with my own kids. I had to get back into their lives, to get back the relationship I lost. I would never call myself a deadbeat dad. I was never that. I was always a part of their lives, but I was not able to contribute the way I wanted to. I did not know how to be a dad. I was full of so much fear, and it cost me the relationship with my kids.

Today I can say that was a good place to start. I needed to fix that first. I remember sitting down with my children, telling them that I can never make up for the lost time. However, I can start from this moment and grow from here. I apologized for missing birthdays, graduations, picnic, barbeques, and so many other things. I told them I would give my level best to be the father they needed and missed.

I then had to learn to be a good brother to my sisters. During my fall from Grace, my brother passed, and that made me feel some type of way. I had to gain the trust of my sisters, showing them that I would be here from now on, being the big brother they desired me to be.

The ultimate challenge was learning to be a son to my parents. When I was going through rough times, my mom and dad stayed true to being parents. It was me who went astray. I stopped being a son, but their love kept me. They never gave up on me.

I was developing a relationship with God. I experienced a lot of spiritual awakenings. Spiritual miracles were happening right before my eyes.

~ He Knows My Name ~

I had a different concept of who I believe God was. I believed God would send me to hell for all the sins I committed. I thought He was a punisher. I had no idea He was just who people said He was, that He was a loving and forgiving God. I learned to repent of my sins and ask for forgiveness. I believed God had washed me of my sins and given me another chance.

God began to show up in my life. He gave me blessings after blessings. He showed me His love. I cannot explain the feeling. One spiritual awareness God showed me was through an old friend of mine. My friend was in the hospital, battling cancer. His name was Mankie. He was a friend from my days of addiction. He was on drugs also. I tell you; this guy was a very sharp dresser. The ladies loved to see him coming. He was a quiet man but smooth as silk.

A few of us made a habit to go and visit him every day. It was hard seeing him this way. There were days he craved for relief from the pain. He knew he had only a brief time, and he asked for drugs to help. I never thought of him being a spiritual man, but he was speaking of God a lot. We visited each day, bringing him food, sitting and talking about the good old days.

One day when we started to leave, he called us back to his bed side and said, "Hey, thanks for all you have been doing for me lately. But do not waste your time coming back here anymore."

I asked, "What do you mean by that?"

My friend said, "Man, last night an angel came to visit me right here in this room. The Lord spoke to me. D, he took me and showed me my resting place. He showed me heaven." He said, "Man, it is beautiful." He talked about streets paved in gold, the water is ever flowing. He told me the angels talked with him. He said he saw a lot of our friends that had gone before him. Mankie said the angel said they would be back to get him. He told us he loved us, and he would see us on the other side one day.

Don and I just looked at each other, and we thought he might have been on some type of drug. I never heard him speak like this before. I had no idea he was spiritual at all.

I asked Don, "Do you think he is on dope?"

Don said, "Naw, man, I do not think he is

 on dope. It does not sound like he is high on anything. That all sounds real."

I leaned over and kissed him on the forehead and told him, "We'll be back tomorrow."

He smiled and nodded. "Take care."

Before we got back to the old neighborhood, we got a call from Mankie's sister. she said, "As soon as you all left, Mankie passed away."

That was my first and closest experience from God. Losing my friend was a sad experience, but God's peace was upon us. I believe my friend knew exactly what he was talking about.

When I look at my life today, I know God speaks to me. He speaks to me in unusual ways. It is not always clear to me sometimes. I understand, yet sometimes I do not. But I will keep searching until it becomes clear to me. I can feel His presence. I know God knows my name. There is no human power that can do what He has done for me. Like relieving me of my addition. I could never do it on my own. I tried and failed, but my God is a deliverer and a strong tower. I was told there is only one who has that power, and today He is my friend. Thank you, Father, for who You are. I am proud to be one of His servants today. I feel like one of His disciples, going out and speaking of His goodness.

Working with the youth, sharing my own testimony, praying, and helping…. I consider myself a walking testimony. Those that knew me back in the day would say I have come a long way, and I do have a story to tell. It will be about all my ups, down, and crazy turn arounds.

~ Chapter 10 ~

The Rise Before the Fall

I soon got a call from one of my childhood friends. He told me he was now living in Orlando, Florida. He is someone I looked up to. I call him my mentor. He was a great athlete, a real smooth guy. He had it going on. He was one of the first guys I knew who made it out of the projects. He is my good friend, Goody.

He said, "Hey, man, why don't you come down here for a few days? Bring your wife and come on down. We can kick back and relax. Don't worry about anything. Don't bring nothing, just yourselves. I would love to see you."

I talked it over with my wife, and we packed up and headed for Orlando. We decided we could enjoy about three days of fun and relaxation.

Goody was a young businessperson; he was involved with a few different things. He lives in an awesome, huge house in a fabulous neighborhood.

I told him, "Man, this a long way from the concrete jungle we lived in before." He told me that God had been good to him. He is on the right track and open to God's blessings.

His home was beautiful, and it was so big. It had a guest house that overlooked a pool. That is where we stayed. Man, it was nice.

~ He Knows My Name ~

One evening, after dinner, my friend and I went by the pool to talk. Our conversations were always positive and meaningful. Goody told me he had been watching me over the years, and he knew I had a mind for business. He said that is an excellent quality to have and to also stay on that path. He also told me to start hanging around successful people, to start going to the best of restaurants. He said, "Just go and sit, and watch how the people interact with each other, watch their body language." He said to go sit in coffee shops. He told me not to be afraid. "Just go and observe. This will give you the desire to move out of the hood slowly but surely."

I thought about what he said, and it made a lot of sense. My wife and I were still living in our one-bedroom apartment. We started looking west. The farther west you lived the better the neighborhood. We got a blessing with the opportunity to move into a two-bedroom apartment. It was a low-income complex with the rent based on our income. My wife was now taking care of her daughter, who was living with us. I always wanted to work at a company called Case Tractor Plant. I am not sure why I chose that particular job. It was weird for me, but it was a better paying job in my community.

Before I could land that job, a film crew came to Racine to film a movie about that particular plant. A friend of mine's wife worked for the company. She called and asked if I wanted to be a stand in for the movie. I said, Sure, I would like to. They were paying $35.00 an hour, so I landed that role. I had to do walk bys. I also got to tour the plant. As I walked through, I said, "This is my dream job."

~ He Knows My Name ~

While I was there, I applied for the job. It took five years to be called, and when the opportunity came, I jumped right on it. After my interview, I never thought in a million years I would land this job. I said to myself after accepting this job, *It is only up from here.*

Now, we were getting our finances together. We were saving, and we finally had enough money to buy my wife a car. One of the things I told my wife when we first got married was that I never wanted her to work. I grew up in a family where the man is the provider. My mom never had to work, and neither would she. My mom took care of the family. My dad was the bread winner.

When we first met, I explained to her that I was not making much money right now, but I am going to do the best I can. I said to my wife, "God is about to open up some doors." I am claiming that victory. I bought my wife her first car. I called her outside and gave her the keys. Pleasing my wife pleases me. I claim that victory.

Life was good. I was sober, making meetings. Blessings were flowing. As a child of God, I do believe we were born to succeed. I am at a point right now where I am experiencing His miracles in my life. It is not about the material things coming. It is the faith I used in receiving them.

It is like the saying "God can do all things but fail." He is a conqueror. It took me a while to truly understand what that really meant. I have seen Him do it for others. I did not believe He would do it for me. Until He started giving me God moments. They began to come into fruition in my life. My visions became real. The blessings continue to flow.

~ He Knows My Name ~

I remember buying my wife a Jaguar, her dream car. She was in love with that car. One day she was looking through a magazine, and she saw a picture of the very same car she dreamed of. She pointed at the picture and said, "This is the one."

I said, "Okay." I took the picture from the magazine and placed it on the refrigerator. It stayed there for over two years. There were times I would walk past the refrigerator and just touch the picture and pray.

One day I was actually looking for a car for myself when, suddenly, I saw my wife's dream car. I looked it over and called the sales agent. After we talked for a while, my mind was made up. I decided to drive over to Chicago to pick it up for her. I told him I needed that car for my wife, and I asked him to wait for me that day. This was a God moment for me. The look on my wife's face when I was able to give her something she always dreamed of was priceless to me.

We were still living in this two-bedroom apartment a little west, into a decent area. I felt we had not reached our goal just yet. A new vision came regarding our desire to own a condo. We had no idea of where it would be or how we were going to get it. There were days when I rode past these units that were being built. It was a beautiful complex. They had swimming pools, and it was gated. As I drove through, I would say, "Wow. One of these days I'm going to live here." I would drive through the complex and watch the buildings go up. I would say, "Yeah, we will live here one day."

One night my wife and I were coming home from dinner, and I took the long way.

~ He Knows My Name ~

She said, "Where are we going? We do not live here."

I said to her, "Not yet we don't." This was another God moment for me. I moved my wife into that condo.

I found myself testing God. I would test his every word. I only had a little faith, but they say you only need faith the size of a muster seed. I kept most of God's blessings to myself. I did not want people to think I was bragging or boasting about what was happening to me. This test was between me and my God. I did not share with anyone, not even my wife. It was based upon my relationship with God. I understood that I had more growing to go; however, I did not want to skip a single lesson. I needed it all step by step. I knew at this moment: God knows my name.

So now it was time for me to pay it forward as an entrepreneur. I teamed up with a good friend of mine who was actually my barber. Leroy and I were walking downtown Racine one day. We stumbled upon a shop for sale. The location was great, and the shop looked great inside. We got the opportunity and grabbed it quick. The downfall was I was not a barber. Leroy had other things he was involved in as well. Our customers did not get the full attention they needed because of our other interests. Well, that did not work out.

Once again, we came together and opened up a drug rehabilitation, sober living home together. That was one of my passions. I always wanted to help others. I needed to be where I could serve people. So, we opened up our first home; however, getting contracted was a lot harder that I thought. Funds ran low, and it became harder to keep that open. My heart was with this program. I kept it in the back of my mind.

~ He Knows My Name ~

I would one day go at this again, whenever I got the opportunity.

I teamed up with one of the Deacons from my Church. I presented the idea to Bob, who is my business partner today. We met one day, and I shared my vision with him. It was that same vision to help others. Bob liked what I had to say. We opened up our first family adult living home together. This was a wonderful experience. We were a good business match, and the bond grew from there. We went on to open our second, our third, and then our fourth home. This became very successful.

I enjoy working with people with disabilities and those that are challenged, just being a part of this is rewarding. I got up close and personal with some of the residents. Some came and stayed. Some came and left when they had to leave. I felt some type of way because I had developed a closeness with them, but I knew they had to move on for the better. Again, God showed me how amazing He is. God knows my name.

In my busyness, I just happened to stumble up on a clothing business, which is today called D's Clothing. Who would have thought I would end up in this business? As much as I love clothes, wow. That business took off like lightening. I was living a dream. I soon picked up a large clientele in the city I lived in. I was now on fire. I was on the move. At the same time, I could not forget where I came from.

At this point, I thought I had to keep busy. Until I ran into a brick wall. It was affecting my household. My wife was always encouraging with some of the things I was involved with. I started putting more time into the business and the outreach ministry. I was doing my thing with the kids. Not realizing I was ignoring her a lot, I thought at that point money would make a difference. I found out it was not about the money for her. My wife told me, "I just want some of your time." I had to reconstruct my life. I downsized a lot of the work I was doing. I started focusing on my marriage. I was blessed to have a supporting God-fearing wife. I had to find balance in my life.

Every morning when I wake up, before I put my feet on the floor, I have to thank God for this new day. For His Grace and His mercy. I do realize He did not have to do it for me. A lot of times I do not feel like I deserve this. I do believe God has a plan for my life. He has shown that to me so far. I always keep a glimpse of my past sitting on my right shoulder to remind me of where I came from. I often have to pinch myself to make sure this is real, that God is really doing what He said He would do for me.

Here I am with a couple of legit business. Things are looking great at this time. My finances are growing. I see more money than I could have ever imagined. All legit this time. Life at this point is well. There are times I have to pinch myself when I look back over my life and see how God has brought me from living in a crack house to owning homes of my own.

Helping people with the same struggles that I overcame in my life amazes me. We serve an amazing God; I thank Him for putting me in a position to help others. He took me through it so I would be able to give, reach out, and help the people going through it now. It gives me joy to be a resource for them.

~ He Knows My Name ~

I remember God saying to me, "Young lad, why are you still walking when I have given you authority to fly?" I know this is a tedious journey. One of the things I had to remember is that I am powerless. I mean powerless over people, places, and things. I had to start watching my feet. At times I would wonder into places I had no business being. There were times I wanted go to back into my old neighborhood just to visit old friends. That old saying always rang in my ear: "If you sit in the barber shop long enough, you will get a haircut." So, I had to be careful whkjlkere I walked. I know on this journey not everybody is for you. Some people are against you.

With the heart that I have, wanting everybody to succeed and feel the goodness of the Lord and His many blessings, I understand that people have to seek God for themselves. One of the biggest mistakes in my life is being a people pleaser. I truly wanted to go back just to lift up a brother or a sister. I found nothing wrong with that. You just have to be careful with doing that. You could very well get pulled down in the process. I had to realize everybody will not be able to go where you are going. What God has for me is for me and what God has for you is yours. Amen! The enemy has been riding my back for so long, but what he meant for evil, my God has worked out in my life, giving me another chance. Amen!

Today I take no credit for any of these blessings. I know God has done for me what I could not do for myself. I understand I did not have the power. Only God has the power to do what He has done. I have always been reminded of those footprints in the sand. I know some of you recognize that old saying. For a long time, I could feel those footprints. I never knew who they belonged to. I can feel them today because I have learned who they belong to. My God carried me. He helped me when I could not help myself. What an awesome God we serve. Amen!

Back then, I never would have imagined this was the rise before my fall. These moments of God happened before all hell broke forth in my life

~ Chapter 11 ~

7th Circle of Hell

One night I was at home. I will never forget this evening. It was on Sunday October 26, 2010. I went to pick up my mom to bring her to spend the night to help celebrate my wife's birthday.

I had gone out that evening to pick up a cake and some ice cream. We were sitting down enjoying the Packers and Vikings game. The game started about 7pm. My Bears had lost, and I was not too happy about that. We did enjoy the cake and ice cream. We even sang happy birthday to my wife.

After the game had gone off, my wife helped my mom get settled into bed. We had planned on getting up the next morning to take my mom back to Chicago. I went upstairs to my bedroom to get my cell phone that had been charging.

As soon as I walked to the phone, it lit up and started to beep. I picked it up. It showed a bunch of missed calls from several family members and friends. I did not hear the rings because the phone was on silent mode.

My sister had called, my aunt, and even the mothers of my kids had called. I said, "What is going on?"

I called my sister. I asked her, "What's going on?" I could hear in her voice that she was upset.

She asked, "Has anybody contacted you yet?"

~ He Knows My Name ~

"I said no. I was watching the game, and I just came upstairs to check to see if the phone was charged up."

"She said you have to get to Chicago. There has been an accident up here. "She asked, is mom still with you?"

I said, "Yeah, she is." I told her mom was okay.

I asked what kind of accident and with who, and she told me with my daughter, Donysha I asked, "Well, what happened?"

She said, "I do not know all the details, but some guy broke intoher house, and things went bad, but you just need to get here quick."

I said, "Just tell me if they are okay."

At this time, they did not want to upset me by telling me what was really going on. They knew I had to drive and that I still had my mom with me. They did not want to upset her.

My sister said, "I will tell you this much. Donysha has been shot."

"Oh, my God," I said. "I'm on my way."

I got some clothes together. I knew my mom had to get back, so we got her things together as well.

My wife asked, "What's going on?"

I told her what my sister had just told me, about the shooting and that my daughter had been hit. I told her I was taking Mom on back with me. I asked my wife to stay home. "I will let you know as soon as I find out more."

~ He Knows My Name ~

At this time, my mom was getting nervous. She wanted to know what was going on. I tried to keep her as calm as possible.

Calls kept coming in as we were driving. My daughter's mom called. She asked, "Are you on your way?

I said, "Yes, I'm in route now."

She said, "I know you heard what happened."

" I said where are the kids?"

" She said hat's another story."

I asked, "Are my kids okay?"

She said, "No." She told me my granddaughter had been shot as well.

I said"Okay." I tried not to answer any more calls.

I will never forget that night. It was raining. The trip was an hour and a half, but it seemed like five hours.

My phone was blowing up, but I tried not to answer. I immediately started praying. I prayed all the way to Chicago, listening to gospel music, just talking to my mom. My mom held my hand during the long trip to Chicago.

I was driving like a bat out of hell. I was trying to get there quick and trying to be safe at the same time.

I pulled up to the hospital. I saw a ton of people standing outside. The news media people were there. Cameras were everywhere. There were so many people I had to search for a parking spot.

~ He Knows My Name ~

People came rushing up to my car. I asked, "Where is she? Where is my daughter?" I looked at the expressions on their faces. I knew it was not good.

They said, "Well…they didn't make it."

I asked, "Who? Who are they?" I was told my daughter didn't make it. She had been killed. My eight year-old granddaughter had been hit six times, and she didn't make it. Her sixteen year-old brother had been hit eight times, and he died at the scene and was still at the house.

I asked, "Where is my four year-old grandson?"

They said he was across town in a trauma unit. He had also been hit seven times, and doctors were working on him.

I went blank. I did not know what was going on. My daughter's mom was trying to get me to go back inside the hospital to identify the body. I refused. I did not want to see my daughter that way.

I needed to get to my grandson who was being operated on across town in another hospital.

I do not remember how I got over there. It was like a flash. I made it to the emergency room to be with my grandson. We were not sure if he would pull through that night. It was pretty horrific.

I ended up going over to my daughter's house that night, back to the scene of crime. I really did not want to be there. People were still there. It was like a war zone.

At this point, which was a lot to take in. My mind was all over the place, and I was feeling overwhelmed. I did not know what to do. I remember walking in the parking lot of the hospital. My grandson was still in surgery. I went out to the parking lot and just started to pray. I did not have any feelings. I was numb.

My next thought was to call my sponsor. I did just that. I called James. I needed to talk to someone. I explained to him what had just happened. It was tough. It was tough even for him to listen. He did not know what to say. But he did offer to come. I said, "No, it's a long drive, and I'm around family." I just needed someone other than family.

He said, "D, I am here, man. Call me at any time." He also said, "Stay close to your family. We will get through this together."

I still had no idea of the details that lead to this point. I went down to the police station to try to get some answers. They were still investigating the case. At that time, they still had no idea of what was really going on.

I titled this chapter "The 7th Circle of Hell" because seven means completion and a circle have no sharp edges or cracks and hell is a place of torment. This experience made me feel as if I was trapped in a place with no way out. No cracks of joy anywhere, and I was in a place of constant torment. I never would have imagined this happening to me in real life. *This only happen in movies*, I thought.

As I stand here today, God has given me a supernatural Grace that has enabled me to move forward in my life. The pain still comes and goes but the Grace of God is yet constant in my life

~ Chapter 12~

Ashes To Ashes and Dust To Dust

The remnants of October 24,2010 are a footprint implanted in my heart and mind forever. I never would have imagined losing my first Daughter Donysha and my first granddaughter Clarisma both at the same time. Pieces of my heart went with them. God allowed me to have 28, almost 29 years with my daughter and 9 years with my granddaughter and I am grateful for those years.

I sit and think often how time has no recovery once it is lost. We cannot get time back. I learned that we may not be able to recover time, but I have learned to redeem the time I have left with my only living daughter, build a relationship with my wife's daughter and our two grandsons. Life has no fury and we do not know what one moment from the next may bring.

This experience has taught me the true meaning of today. I am in awe of the scripture *Proverbs 6:4 NLT Don't put it off; do it now! Don't rest until you do.* Time is of essence for me. I am intentional in everything I do. I am intentional with my love, my business affairs, and most of all my walk with the Lord. There is a song I am reminded of by Timothy Wright that simply says, "You brought me through this, you brought me through that, Lord I am grateful to you. You made a way out of no way, you turned my midnights into day, Lord I am so grateful to you."

~ He Knows My Name ~

The process of putting my broken pieces back together after losing my daughter and granddaughter was very hard. It took everything within me not lose my sobriety that I had fought so very hard to maintain. I knew the pain of losing my sobriety in time past because of triggers. I had to really gather myself and lean strongly on God and on my support system in order not to fall back again.

I had to call on the God that I had come to know, and He came to know me. I had to rely on the strength of my yesterdays. I had to remember the time I was addicted to crack, and He delivered me and set me free. I had to remember when He took the taste of alcohol from me, and I am standing in my sobriety today.

I had to take a trip down memory lane and reflect on all the things God has done in my life. I knew this was a different type of test, and I had never been through this level of grief before. What I did know is the same God that brought me out yesterday is the same God that would bring me out of this. It was time for me to fall on my face before God and let Him know it will be Him and only Him to bring me out of this hell, I found myself in.

It took a lot of healing and continued weekly meetings to maintain my sobriety. I had many thoughts of going back, but I had to remember my why and held on. I did not back slide. I was strengthened. I am here as a living testament of God's amazing Grace. It is truly a day-by-day process for me.

It has been over a decade since this happened, and we are yet in the courts to bring justice. None the less, God said in *Romans 12:19 KJV, "Dearly beloved, avenge not yourselves, but rather give place unto wrath: for it is written, Vengeance is mine; I will repay, saith the Lord."*

I know you are wondering how can I allow God to take the vengeance on this senseless, heartless, hurtful, unforgettable tragedy I experienced in my life? I am so glad you asked. Well as I went down my memory lane, I remembered all the God moments I experienced. God begin to remind me that he is the same God yesterday, today and will be the same God tomorrow and forever more. He does not change. If he did it before, he will do it again. He let me know that everything I had encountered he would turn it around and cause it to work for my good.

My relationship with the Father has strengthened. I never knew the Grace of God the way that I know it now. When I was able to resolve within myself, I was able to bring closure to my pain. When I was able to say, Ashes to Ashes and Dust to Dust, God poured in the oil and the wine. God said in his word in *Isaiah 61:3 KJV "To appoint unto them that mourn in Zion, to give unto them beauty for ashes, the oil of joy for mourning, the garment of praise for the spirit of heaviness, that they might be called trees of righteousness, the planting of the Lord, that He might be glorified."*

According to google, the ancient symbol of the tree has been found to represent physical, and spiritual nourishment, transformation and liberation, union, and fertility.

Isaiah 61:3 NIV version states "They will be called oaks of righteousness, a planting of the LORD for the display of his splendor."

~ He Knows My Name ~

This particular version brings out the type of tree God was comparing our strength to once he brought us out of a mourning period. I can truly say, what I have encountered in my lifetime, has strengthened me. I am able to endure hardness like a soldier. I am not so easily shaken. I definitely do not sweat the small stuff.

As God compares our strength as an Oak Tree in Isaiah 61:3 NIV, research has shown the mighty Oak Tree has long been a symbol of endurance, durability, strength, and longevity. The roots of Oak Tree runs deep and wide. It is said an Oak Tree can withstand serious storms and is not easily shaken by the toughest of winds.

When you go through deep waters, I will be with you. When you go through rivers of difficulty, you will not drown. When you walk through the fire of oppression, you will not be burned up; The flames will not consume you. Isaiah 43:2 NLT

There were many days I felt like oh death would swallow me up. I felt like a dead man walking. There were many days I thought the storms would never stop raging in my life. Depression was aimed to take my mind. I battled daily with the what if's and the why's. Yes, I questioned God. I needed to know why he allowed something so tragic to happen all at once. This was a tough pill to swallow. I had to take those pills in doses. God had to help me process that tragedy day by day. It was too much to take in all at once.

I went through stages of grief. When it all occurred, I went numb and was in denial. I was not able to immediately identify the body. I knew if I identified it was my daughter and granddaughter, I had to accept they were dead. That was too much. Accepting their death was the hardest step in my grieving process.

After I accepted, they were truly gone, the anger came. I was angry mostly at myself. I just felt I did not protect her. I was angry at the person's involved because they took innocent lives. I was angry at the Lord because how could he allow something of this caliber to happen to both my babies.

I went into a stage of telling God, I would do whatever it took if they could just come back. Take me in their place. I just wanted all this to be a nightmare and I just wanted to wake up and someone say it was all a dream. That never happened.

When my anger turned inward and I knew I was helpless, depression set in. Life was never the same. It was hard for a while to get going. I had my businesses, my wife, and my other daughter that needed me to pull myself up out of that depressed state. I battled losing my sobriety daily. It was a fight to hold on to what I fought so hard to maintain. Life did not look the same for me. I never imagined me burying my daughter let along my granddaughter. This was mind blowing to me.

God never left my side. My wife and family never left my side. I had to remember they were hurting also. I had to remember we were all grieving their loss. God gave me a prayer of serenity to start praying over my life daily. This is when I came to acceptance.

I Prayed

God

grant me the

Serenity

to accept the things

I cannot change, the

Courage

To change the things

I can, and the

Wisdom

To know the

difference.

Reinhold Niebuhr

~ He Knows My Name ~

I had to learn to go on with my life in their absence. I would forever hold their memory in my heart. It is not a day that go by, I do not think of them. This book is so very important to me because it was when I accepted their loss, God revealed to me a knowing of who he truly was. He sent many things to help me get through the dark days in my life, one being Tasha Cobb song, "He Knows My Name" The part that says, "No fire can burn me, No battle can turn me, No mountain can stop me, because you hold my hand." Yes, that part. He walked me through the fire, through the battle and over every mountain.

I often compare my life to jobs. Things were going so well when this tragedy happened. God was blessing me like non other. I was prospering in every aspect of my life. I never would have imagined my life as a entrepreneur and business man with several streams of income. The tragedy happened so fast and unexpected. It was like a domino affect when I was told, My daughter, my granddaughter, her brother was all deceased and my grandson was fighting for his life. It was a Job moment in my life.

I had purposed in my heart no matter what, I had to maintain my integrity. Though he slay me, yet will I trust in him: but I will maintain mine own ways before him. Job 13:15 KJV

Quotes That Depict My Journey

"You will get through this. It won't be painless. It won't be quick. But God will use this mess for good. In the meantime, don't be foolish or naïve. But don't despair either. With God's help you (me) will get through this."

Max Lucado

Happy Moments,

Praise God.

Difficult Moments

Seek God.

Quite Moments,

Worship God.

Painful Moments,

Trust God.

Every Moments,

Thank God.

Amen.

Daily Inspirational Quotes

God has not forgotten you.

You will bounce-back from every

Setback and negative situation you

Are experiencing. Your story has

already been written. Your final scene

has been shot. You don't end in

failure. You end in victory!

Christ Religious Inspirational Quote

Conclusion

As I conclude this journey of my life, I want to end with A Prayer, Being Observant, A Reflection, Balance, Keys and Gratefulness. This journey I experienced is surreal, and if you do not truly know, I am a living witness and a testament of the realness of God. After a lengthy battle with addictions and a traumatic experience of great loss, it took God and His amazing Grace to pull me through. He did not just pull me through, but He gave me double for my trouble. God placed favor on my life, and what I went through is not in vain. God knows my name. My name is now written in the lamb's book of Life. I know Him, and we commune together. It took a lot for me to come to the end of myself and come full circle. I would never wish this experience on anyone, but I can say now I have a measure of understanding. I did not allow this journey to make me bitter. Everything I went through made me better. I conclude with me admonishing anyone who can relate to my journey to reach out, and I will be willing to mentor and help you get through your rough spots. I admonish you to have a personal relationship with God and allow Him to help you in any and every way.

Prayer

Lord God, you are the God of wisdom and truth. You are the creator of all Wisdom. Lord, make me wise. You have set responsibilities before me, and I want to do them well. Give me wisdom in every task You have set before me. I know that you can never have too much wisdom. So, make me wise. Help me to fulfill my purpose while I am still on this side of the earth. It took me going through many peaks and valleys to realize You know me. You know every hair I had and have on my head. You know the stars, and You call them all by name. You know the pebbles by the seashore, and You also know my name. You have given me abilities and gifts to use for your glory, and I say, "Thank you, Lord." Always keep me humble because I do not want to be proud. I want to always remember from whence You have brought me. You said in Your word You give Grace to the humble and You resist the proud. I am forever indebted to You for always covering me with your Grace and mercy. I pray that whoever crosses my path that has had to deal with additions and grief, give me the words to speak and allow my life to speak for You. I come to You in Jesus' name, amen.

Being Observant

No matter how far you try to overcome your darkest days in your life or try to change, there will always be a group of people that will always see you the way you were before, not as the person you have become.

Well, today my swag has not changed, but my spirit has. What do I mean by that? Take this, for example. I remember going to a family reunion back in Chicago. I came across one of my cousins, and we just so happened to be talking about good times. One of my aunts walked up and said, "Did you know that Dyland was a Deacon?"

My other cousin looked at me and said, "No I did not. You do not look like a Deacon." She asked when this happened.

I said, "It's been about two years now."

She stood back and looked me up and down and said, "You don't look like a Deacon."

I said, "What does a deacon look like?"

She said, "Not you."

I will never forget what she said.

You see, that is just what I mean. All she could see was the old D. People will always judge you on who you were before, and on your outer appearance, instead of the inner you. This is sad but true. I was a little offended by that. I soon got over it. I consider it a lesson learned.

Balance

So, now we are talking about balance, something I had no clue about. Trying to balance my life. I was staying close to the people that mattered: my wife, my kids, and my family. One of the other things I had to watch out for was being grandiose or getting the big head. I noticed I have to remain humble at all times and not forget where I came from. So, I am really enjoying the fruits and the benefits of God's miracles.

One time I was getting the big head, thinking I was all that and a bag of chips I do remember that old saying: "Be careful because the same people you pass going up the ladder, you see them coming down." I want to make sure I do right by others, treating everybody with respect for who and where they are. It was by God's Grace and mercy, that I am where I am. What an awesome God we serve, amen!

Keys

Let us stop here for a moment and talk about keys. That is right. I said keys.

So, the way I am living now, hearing all these things about doing the right thing would have sounded foreign to me back in the day. However, today I have keys in my life. I have my own set of keys to my car. I have my own set of keys to my home.

I am no longer knocking on doors, trying to get in, having people look through the peep hole, seeing it is me and wondering if they should let me in, hoping I will turn and walk away. I have my own keys today to my own doors.

Words of Wisdom

Proverbs 4:6-7
King James Version

6 Forsake her not, and she shall preserve thee: love her, and she shall keep thee.

7 Wisdom is the principal thing; therefore get wisdom: and with all thy getting get understanding.

According to google the meaning of wisdom is having the ability to make good judgments based on what you have learned from your experience, or the knowledge and understanding that gives you this ability.

I can truly say, I have not only gained experience on my journey, but I have also gained knowledge and understanding. Grace Quote said it best "You cannot lead people where you have never been. You cannot impart what you do not possess. You cannot preach with power what you are not practicing with integrity."

It took many relapses for me to truly realize what I was dealing with was a disease and I needed the same type of help a person that was dealing with a physical illness needed but in a different area of expertise. My sickness was not physical. I had areas of my life that was sick that medicine could not cure. My sickness was nothing a test result would determine how to proceed with the best course of action that is best for the type of disease I had. No, no, no. It took a deeper measure of help for me.

With my experience came knowledge. Knowledge is having the facts, information and the skills through experience or education. When I made the decision to accept help, I checked myself into a program that was skilled with dealing with people who suffered with addictions. The first step in my process was admitting I was an addict. The second step was to admit I needed help. Once I could do those two steps, I then could accept the education that I received about my disease. I learned so much about perception and having a psychic change. I had to learn how to shift my thinking. I learned as long as I thought like an addict, my actions would follow. I had to see myself walking in my sobriety as a sober man being able to contribute to society before, I actually got there. I had to see myself there and then start walking towards it.

I know you thinking, that is easy peasy? Well it was not an easy rode for me. After some failed attempts, I began to think this was no doable and I was losing hope. What I loved about the program is I had a community that surrounded me when I came to that hopeless place within the process. They did not judge me, we were in this together. I could be free to express my true feelings. I did not have a need to want to fake the funk. I had no reason to have to pretend to be something other than who and what I was. When times got really hard, I knew I could express how I was feeling in our meetings. By the end of the meeting, I could feel my hope building momentum. Over time my whole mental, emotional, and spiritual being shifted within my entire perception of who I was becoming.

I learned on this journey to surround myself with like-minded people. Who I hung out with had a great impact on holding true to my sobriety. I was given words of wisdom often about not visiting my old spots that I would hang out and get alcohol and drugs. I was told, it was too soon. I did not understand that then, but I listened, and I am so glad I did. As time progressed, I did not desire to return to those places to hang out anymore. My heart shifted to go back to help as many people as possible that too suffered with addictions. That is when that understanding came into play.

~ He Knows My Name ~

I can have empathy for those who are like I once was. I can look in their eyes and see the pain and suffering. I can empathize when I see the blank stares of hopelessness. That was me one day. I can empathize to the point of sharing my testimony with them to let them see, there is hope. I understand them because they were one day me. If you have never experienced addiction, you cannot truly understand another person that suffers with that disease. Many addicts sit on the other side of judgment. People say things like "how could they use their food money to buy drugs/alcohol and now begging for food?"

People on the outside looking in do not understand the overwhelming feeling that takes over one's mind and appetite as an addict. All you do is breathe and live to drink or get a fix. I understand the triggers, and the withdrawals. I understand the late-night sweats and shakes when you purposed in your heart you were going to stop using and drinking. I understand the disappointment I put on the faces of those I loved that had high hopes for me to recover and be a better person in society. I understand all of that. I went through the valley of the shadow of death before I made a conscious decision to fight for my life.

~ He Knows My Name ~

I have learned to see life from 2 set of eyes. I have been on both sides of the spectrum. I can get down in the mud with you if you are still struggling with addiction and I can walk amongst the greatest. I am like Paul when he said in Philippians 4:11–13. KJV

11 Not that I speak in respect of want: for I have learned, in whatsoever state I am, therewith to be content.

12 I know both how to be abased, and I know how to abound: everywhere and in all things am instructed both to be full and to be hungry, both to abound and to suffer need.

13 I can do all things through Christ which strengtheneth me.

~ He Knows My Name ~

Story of Reflection

One winter day, I was shoveling outside my condo complex. My neighbor, Mrs. Rogers, walked up to me and said, "Hey, D, we will be leaving for Florida, and we will be gone for about a month." She asked if she could leave her keys with me to go over and check on her apartment while she would be away.

I turned and looked at her.

She said, "All I need you to do is check in and make sure everything is okay."

I felt really appreciated. I said, "Sure, Mrs. Rogers. I can do that for you."

As she walked away, I just stood there for a moment with the shovel in my hand. I thought, *Wow! People are really trusting me today with keys to their homes.* I said, "Okay. This is great."

A week later my neighbor to the right side of me, Ms. Annie, knocked on the door. She asked if me and my wife could keep a set of keys to her house and look after her dog while she is at work.

I said, "Sure. Okay."

Shortly after that, I was at a church meeting, where I was meeting with the other Deacons. During the meeting, Pastor walked up to me and handed me a set of keys to the church.

I said, looking at God, "Wow. Okay!"

~ He Knows My Name ~

Soon after that, my employer promoted me to be assistant manager, and he handed me a set of keys to the store. What trust! I was thinking to myself, *If they only knew who I used to be, what I used to do.* They must all have seen something in me that was becoming clear to me. The word of God says you will stand out amongst many, and your light will forever shine. One of the things in life I try to do is to be careful of judging. I try hard not to judge anybody.

My brother, Robert, may his soul rest in peace. He passed away in 1993 as a result of AIDS. I came to find out later that my brother was gay. That shocked the family. He started out being straight. He had a girlfriend. Things were good until they were not anymore. Things started to turn weird on us. He started hanging out with gay guys, telling us that they were only friends and that he was not that way. Later he came out, breaking the news, and told my mom. My mom told my dad, and neither of them welcomed that news. That was a hard pill for us all to swallow, especially me.

My brother and I were like night and day. We had totally different lifestyles. My brother was a smart young man, always had his head in a book. I was this street guy, always doing worldly things. I kept my head in the streets. When we got the news of him being gay, he had gotten infected with HIV from one of his partners. For a while, I did not want to accept that. I passed judgement on that situation and him. It was a very painful feeling, watching my brother go through this agonizing experience.

At the time, there was no medication to treat the disease, but the family came to terms with it, and we dealt with it like a family. We became very forgiving, knowing that he was our brother and my parents' son. Robert went on to be with Lord, and I was so glad I made peace with him before he passed on. Even after that, I became more homophobic. As my walk with the Lord grew stronger, I overcame my fear of same sex. I thought about how some people would judge me regarding my past, so who am I to judge anyone? Today I know who I am.

Gratefulness

I am in a very good place in my life. I have reaped the goodness of the Lord, enjoying the fruits of my laboring.

God has been extra, extra good to me. I am full of gratitude I have been blessed with so many gifts from above.

Now, I remember some nights I would lay down to rest, and I would begin to talk to my God, thanking Him for all He has done for me. I would lay and bask in His glory.

I reflect back of all the events that took place in my life. I recall to my mind the faithfulness of my God. I think about my support system: my wife and family, church family, and all the people God has placed in my life as mentors and all the people He placed in my life to mentor.

Lord, if You do not ever do anything else for me, You have done more than I could ever dream of. You have exceeded my thinking and believing. Lord, I thank You; I thank You for everything, including this new life You have given me.

Going Down Memory Lane

WHERE IT ALL STARTED!

Dyland at 14   Robert Weather Sr. Robert Jr. & Dyland

HOW IT IS GOING NOW!

~ He Knows My Name ~

Psalm 23: 1-6
King James Version

1 The LORD is my shepherd; I shall not want.

2 He maketh me to lie down in green pastures: he leadeth me beside the still waters.

3 He restoreth my soul: he leadeth me in the paths of righteousness for his name's sake.

4 Yea, though I walk through the valley of the shadow of death, I will fear no evil: for thou art with me; thy rod and thy staff they comfort me.

5 Thou preparest a table before me in the presence of mine enemies: thou anointest my head with oil; my cup runneth over.

6 Surely goodness and mercy shall follow me all the days of my life: and I will dwell in the house of the LORD for ever.

Dyland Weather
Biography

https://www.facebook.com/dyland.weather?mibextid=LQQJ
4d

Dylandweather@yahoo.com

Dyland Weather was born in Chicago IL, south-side on June
5, 1962, to Robert and Nina Weather. Dyland grew up in a
family of six, two brothers and two sisters, and our parents.
Dyland two sisters are Lisa Weather and Wendy Weather.
Dyland late brother is Robert Weather Jr.

Dyland met the love of his life Barbara Weather and they
have been married for 19 years. Dyland has one living
daughter Delilah Weather and one deceased daughter

~ He Knows My Name ~

Donysha Tovell. Dyland has two grandsons Michael Weather and Nathaniel Davis and one deceased granddaughter Clarisma Torrey. Dyland has one stepdaughter named Lakisha Lockridge. Dyland and his wife Barbara now reside in Racine Wisconsin.

Dyland's deceased daughter and granddaughter is the motivation factor behind him writing this book. He writes it in their honor and dedicate every word on every page to them. Dylands life mission is to keep their memory alive and seek full justice for their tragic untimely deaths. He will forever hold them near and dear to his heart.

Dyland has dedicated his life to business as an entrepreneur and ministry as a mentor and a deacon. Dyland has several businesses, and he has given a safe place for kids that are at risk and help mentor them to walk the right path. Dyland has set a blaze in his community as a Philanthropist that donates his time, money, experiences, skills and gifts to help create a better world for others.

Dyland went from trying times to transition, and from transition to transforamtion, and from transformation to tragedy and from tragedy to triumph. Dyland did all of that leaning and depending on the one true and Living God. Within all of these seasons, what kept Dyland on the straight and narrow, and clothe him in his right mind, is his personal relationship with the Lord. Dyland has not only dedicated his life to serve others, first and foremost he has dedicated his life to Christ Jesus as savior, Lord, and King.

My Book of Memories
Me, Grandmother and My Parents

Me, Children and Grandchildren

~ He Knows My Name ~

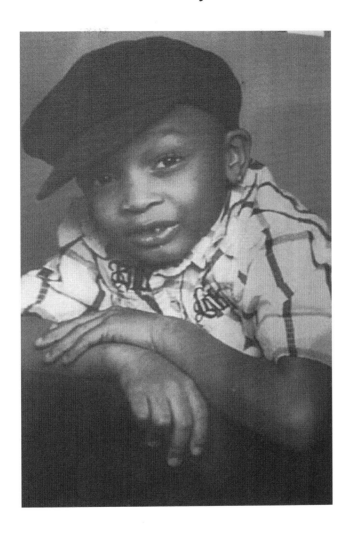

~ He Knows My Name ~

~ He Knows My Name ~

~ He Knows My Name ~

~ He Knows My Name ~

~ He Knows My Name ~

Family and Friends

~ He Knows My Name ~

~ He Knows My Name ~

~ He Knows My Name ~

~ He Knows My Name ~

~ He Knows My Name ~

~ He Knows My Name ~

~ He Knows My Name ~

My Saving Grace, Tux and Sadie

~ He Knows My Name ~

~ He Knows My Name ~

~ He Knows My Name ~

~ He Knows My Name ~

Made in United States
Troutdale, OR
03/28/2024

18760409R00084